A
SELECTION OF
CONTEMPORARY RELIGIOUS
POETRY

A
Selection of
Contemporary Religious
Poetry

Compiled
by
Samuel Hazo

(An Original Deus Book)

DEUS BOOKS
PAULIST PRESS
(Paulist Fathers)
Glen Rock, N.J.

To the Faculty and Students

of

Duquesne University

Cover Design by Claude Ponsot

Cover Photo of Dr. Samuel Hazo by James P. Blair.

Library of Congress Catalog Card Number: 63-23211

Published by the Paulist Press
Editorial Office: 401 W. 59th St., N.Y. 19, N.Y.
Business Office: Glen Rock, New Jersey

Manufactured in the
United States of America

ACKNOWLEDGMENTS

For the permission to reprint the copyrighted material in this volume the editor's grateful thanks are due to the following:

ATHENEUM PUBLISHERS for "Angel" from *Water Street* © 1960, 1961, 1962 by James Merrill

ANDRE DEUTSCH, LTD. for "'What If The World Were a Horrible Mad Fit . . .'" and "In Memoriam C. W." from *The Gravel Ponds* by Peter Levi, S.J.

DODD, MEAD & COMPANY for "Before There Was No Reason in the World" from *The Sorrows of Cold Stone* © 1951 by John Malcolm Brinnin

DOUBLEDAY AND COMPANY, INC. for "God Germed in Raw Granite" from *The Hazards of Holiness* © 1962 by Brother Antoninus; "On a Child Who Lived One Minute" from *Nude Descending a Staircase* © 1958 by X. J. Kennedy

ALAN DUGAN for "Holiday" from *Poems* published by Yale University Press

E. P. DUTTON & CO., INC. for "Personal Letter to the Ephesians" and "The Good Earth" from *The Man Behind You* © 1959 by Carl Bode

FARRAR, STRAUS & COMPANY, INC. for "Lachrymae Christi" and "Miserere" from *Celebration at Dark* by William Jay Smith; "Lines: I Praise God's Mankind in an Old Woman" from *Friday's Child* by Wilfred Watson

THE FIDDLEHEAD for "Who Does Not Understand" from *Emu, Remember!* by Alfred W. Purdy, © and published by the University of New Brunswick

HARCOURT, BRACE & WORLD, INC. for "Christmas Eve under Hooker's Statue," "Children of Light" and "The Holy Innocents" from *Lord Weary's Castle* © 1944, 1946 by Robert Lowell; "On Saint Theresa's Difficulty in Keeping Her Feet on the Ground" © 1959 by Ned O'Gorman from his book, *The Night of the Hammer* and "Reading Dante with Ionians" and "A Homage to My Jewish Students at Christmas Time" © by Ned O'Gorman from his book *Adam Before His Mirror;* "Love Calls Us to the Things of This World," "Philippe de Thaun: The Pelican" and "An Event" from *Things of This World* © 1956 by Richard Wilbur

HARPER & ROW, PUBLISHERS, INC. for "Living in Sin" from *The Diamond Cutters* © 1954 by Adrienne Rich Conrad

HOUGHTON MIFFLIN COMPANY for "Roosters" and "The Prodigal" from *Poems: North and South, A Cold Spring* by Elizabeth Bishop; "Timeo" and "Cock A'Hoop" from *Birthdays from the Ocean* by Isabella Gardner; "To Christ Our Lord" and "Easter" from *What a Kingdom It Was* by Galway Kinnell; "Water Ouzel" from

Water Ouzel by William H. Matchett; "For God While Sleeping" from *All My Pretty Ones* by Anne Sexton and "Unknown Girl in the Maternity Ward" from *To Bedlam and Part Way Back* by Anne Sexton

Indiana University Press for "A Widow in Wintertime" from *The Ungrateful Garden* by Carolyn Kizer

Margot Johnson Agency *for* "Boom" and "Moment" from *New and Selected Poems* by Howard Nemerov © 1960 and published by the University of Chicago Press

Alfred A. Knopf, Inc. for "Notre Dame de Chartres" © 1957 by William Meredith and "A Korean Seated by a Wall" © 1956 by William Meredith from his book *The Open Sea;* "Revisit to the Room of a Saint" © 1961 by John Logan from his book *Spring of the Thief*

John Logan for "Cycle for Mother Cabrini" from *Cycle for Mother Cabrini* published by Grove Press

The Macmillan Company for "The Crucifix" and "Loneliness" from *Time Without Number* © 1952, 1957 by Daniel Berrigan; "Tourist in Dante" from *The Word Is Love* by Sister M. Maura, S.S.N.D. © 1958 by The Macmillan Company; "Friday So Soon "and "The Blue Tree" from *Collected Poems, 1937-1962* by Winfield Townley Scott © 1949, 1950, 1951, 1953, 1954, 1956 1957, 1959 by The Macmillan Company

The Marvell Press (England) for "Church Going" from *The Less Deceived* by Philip Larkin

Samuel Menashe for "O Many Named Beloved" and "There Is No Jerusalem but This" from *The Many Named Beloved* published by Victor Gollanz, Ltd. (England)

New Directions, Publishers for "The Jacob's Ladder" and "The Thread" from *The Jacob's Ladder* © 1958, 1961 by Denise Levertov Goodman; "Evening: Zero Weather" from *Figures for an Apocalypse* by Thomas Merton © 1947 by New Directions, Publishers, and "For My Brother Reported Missing in Action, 1943 from *Thirty Poems* by Thomas Merton © 1944 by Our Lady of Gethsemani Monastery

THE NEWMAN PRESS for "For a Seventy-fifth Birthday," "The Day My Father Was Buried" and "Over Elements" from *The Linen Bands* by Raymond Roseliep

OXFORD UNIVERSITY PRESS, INC. for "The Horse Chestnut Tree" and "The Fury of Aerial Bombardment" from *Collected Poems, 1930-1960* © 1960 by Richard Eberhart

RUTGERS UNIVERSITY PRESS for "Elegy for Sandro" from *As If* by John Ciardi © 1955 by the Trustees of Rutgers College in New Jersey

CHARLES SCRIBNER'S SONS for "Tree of Blame" © 1955 by Norma Farber and "While Eve" © 1954 by Norma Farber from her book *The Hatch;* "The Man Who Married Magdalene" © 1951 by Louis Simpson from his book *Good News of Death;* "Order of Diet" © 1957 by May Swenson from her book *To Mix With Time*

SHEED & WARD, INC. for "Graveyard" from *Testament and Other Poems* by John Fandel © 1959 by Sheed & Ward, Inc.; "Postscript to Many Letters," "To My Mother" and "The Encounter" from *The Quiet Wars* by Samuel Hazo © 1962 by Sheed & Ward, Inc.

WILLIAM SLOANE ASSOCIATES for "Love Poem" and "Letter" from *The Iron Pastoral* © 1947 by John Frederick Nims

ALAN SWALLOW, PUBLISHER for "The Virgin Mary" from *The Form of Loss* © 1956 by Edgar Bowers; "The Wandering Scholar's Prayer to St. Catherine of Egypt" from *The Exclusions of a Rhyme: Poems and Epigrams* © 1960 by J. V. Cunningham; "Epitaph below a Crucifix" from *The Battlement* © 1956 by Donald F. Drummond

UNIVERSITY OF NOTRE DAME PRESS for "Montoya in Exile" and "Dirge for a New Mexican Prelate" from *Sand Verbena* by Suzanne Gross; "Last Things," "Children of Men" and "Paternity" from *Children and Older Strangers* by Ernest Sandeen

UNIVERSITY OF PITTSBURGH PRESS for "Stones" and "Night" from *The Stone and the Shell* by Sara Henderson Hay

PETER VIERECK for "Mount Athos" from *Terror and Decorum* published by Charles Scribner's Sons

THE VIKING PRESS, INC. for "Letter from a Distant Land" from *Letter from a Distant Land* © 1955, 1957 by Philip Booth; "Christmas in Whitneyville" from *The Dark Houses* © 1958 by Donald Hall; "Conversation in Avila" and "Six Nuns in the Snow" from *Times Three* © 1954 by Phyllis McGinley

WESLEYAN UNIVERSITY PRESS for "A Lullaby" © 1956 by Barbara Howes and "The Nuns Assist at Childbirth" © 1954 by Barbara Howes from her book *Light and Dark;* "No Return" and "Paradox" from *Wage War on Silence* © 1956 by Vassar Miller

THE WORLD PUBLISHING CO. for "Saint Ann" from *Encounters* by Daniel Berrigan, S.J.

YALE UNIVERSITY PRESS for "Fable Blackboard" and "Worship" from *Bone Thoughts* by George Starbuck; "Father," "Come Forth" and "Mutterings Over the Crib of a Deaf Child" from *The Green Wall* by James Wright

CONTENTS

INTRODUCTION

In *Creative Intuition in Art and Poetry,* Jacques Maritain has written that "it is difficult for a modern poet not to be a child of modern man." If this statement is even partially true, and if modern man, as we are reminded to the point of cliché, lives in a culture that contains within itself the seeds of its own disintegration, it would seem inevitable that poets would be compelled to face this crisis. Their poetry would in some way reflect the tension created by the necessity of integration on the one hand and the deflecting forces of disintegration on the other. Such a conflict has created an age of anxiety, containment or austerity, depending upon whether one chooses the noun of W. H. Auden, R. W. B. Lewis or Marguerite Higgins. And the impact of anxiety, containment and austerity has created the inescapable challenges that mid-century poets have had to face in creating a poetry in contact with its time.

Since every poet must face the facts of life within his own age before he can refuse, accept or transcend them, it is interesting to note how mid-century poets—primarily in America—have done so, and it is equally interesting to note how the resources of Christianity have helped them to do so. I am speaking now of those poets (and certainly not all of them) who have written during the forties, the fifties and the early sixties. Moreover, I speak of a spirit or vision incarnated in their poetry and not of any supra-literary allegiance paid by any of them to a particular orthodoxy.

Basic to the observations that will follow is one of the poet's fundamental disciplines: that he must see clearly before he can express or interpret, consciously or instinctively, what he has seen. The poet begins, as Mark Van Doren has noted, with the facts of life, as opposed, for instance, to the scientist, who ends with them. I choose to identify this expression of what a poet sees or begins with as the poetry of contact. To put it another way, the poetry of contact is a way of describing the expression of poetic vision in relation to its time.

There are basically three possible results of this type of contact—retreat, engagement or transcendence. The poetry of retreat is a poetry characterized by disgust, aversion or a number of symptoms of escape. The poetry of engagement attempts to affirm and capture the passing world of fact simply as phenomena. The poetry of transcendence is written by one who is able to see within and beyond the point of contact in an evaluative or interpretive way. But all three of these alternatives begin with contact.

The poetry of retreat is really a poetry of refusal. Almost all of the best mid-century poetry which confronts the more unpalatable aspects of contemporary life has something of the poetry of retreat about it. But not all such poetry is able to rise above this. Indeed, one of the misfortunes of some contemporary talents is their inability to rise above their own negativism. Much Beat poetry reveals this negativism. The failure of such poetry, which is often erratically brilliant, is that its writers have orgied in their own disappointment and chagrin. They have made contact; they have seen, and often quite clearly, but they have salvaged little from such contact beyond indignation, disgust and, at times, self-pity.

Of the Beats, Gene Feldman has written that "the Square has his suburbia with a picture window looking out over a graveyard, or he kids himself by chalking political slogans on subway stations. But the man who is Beat knows that he is alone, and that his problem is to learn to live with this knowledge. As a consequence, his concern is primarily one of self-exploration, of perceiving the self in terms of its connection with immediate experience. Not capable of the act of faith required by a belief in tomorrow, the Beat Man values relationships only as they tend to reveal the truth of his present existence."

Without going into the sociological implications of this credo, it seems to me that its negativism is apparent. By denying the possibility of an act of faith in tomorrow, which is not necessarily the chronological tomorrow nor a bigger-

and-better tomorrow, the Beat poet disrupts the continuity of life itself. Despite his possible claims to the contrary, he goes from being anti-society to being anti-life. His poetry often becomes a form of intellectual nudism. And occasionally he resolves his dilemma in the manner of the final act of a nihilistic play—by bitterness, breakdown, loss of mind, loss of hope.

But the poetry of retreat is not only exemplified by some of the Beat poets, who have more or less already passed from the literary scene. It may also manifest itself when poets retreat into phrase or mere word-play, or into a type of personal mystique or highly personal vocabulary bristling with recondite symbolism. I am not necessarily condemning these things, which for some poets are necessary I suppose, but only indicating some of the symptoms of poetry when it is not able to maintain contact.

The poetry of engagement attempts to affirm and capture the world of fact. In simplest terms, it is a poetry that is able to hold its ground before the moment without really interpreting it in an evaluative way. It is concerned with simple seizure, with holding the line. The poet's principal concern is to testify to the moment with which he is in contact. He simply wishes to remain in contact, in a one-dimensional if not a multi-dimensional way.

The poetry of transcendence exceeds and fulfills the poetry of engagement in much the same way in which union exceeds and fulfills desire, or communion exceeds and fulfills aspiration. It results when a poet sees *through* as well as *with* the eye, to borrow the language of William Blake. What makes this possible is that the poet's capacity for love enables him to transmute the poetry of engagement into the poetry of transcendence. This love, suffusing his poetic vision, drives the poet to see within and beyond the point of contact; it rinses the eye so that what is seen appears without distortion. It creates the climate for evaluative expression and for the articulation of what is biblically called prophetic vision or for what Gerard Manley Hopkins described in his theory of "inscape." It is directly related to Jacques Maritain's definition of poetry as the "divination of the spiritual in the things of sense," and it is in part a fulfillment of what T. S. Eliot

alluded to in the thirties when he somewhat hopefully antici-
pated a literature that "would be unconsciously, rather than
deliberately and defiantly, Christian."

The poetry of transcendence is truly a "divination," and
some of the poets of this century have shown an understanding of this. Hart Crane, for example, realized this when he
wrote in 1929 that modern poetry should be based "on the
articulation of the contemporary human consciousness *sub
specie aeternitatis,* and inclusive of all readjustments incident
to science and other shifting factors related to that consciousness." The poets whose work is included in this anthology
seem to me to show a similar awareness. The poems that I
have selected are those that reveal a religious or transcendent
sensibility, *i.e.,* an ability to see beneath the surface of things
sub specie aeternitatis. This has been my basic criterion of
selection, and I have deliberately concentrated on poets of
the forties, fifties and early sixties because I believe that
their poems should be brought to the attention of the poetry-
reading public. The poets of an earlier generation have already been most generously and frequently anthologized, and
there seemed little justification to repeat what has already
been done—and done quite well—by other editors.

My principal reason for speaking of the poetry of retreat,
engagement and transcendence has been to suggest the three
dominant strains that I detect in the work of most modern
poets and to place the poetry of transcendence in its proper
perspective. I have been inclined to call poems transcendent
which reveal a vision suffused by something akin to love. As
a poet lacks love (and the hope and faith that it engenders),
to the extent of his lack is he forced to retreat. As he pos-
sesses love, so is he able to confront and at least affirm in
a purely objective way the world before him. His poetry may
not ascend, but it does not fall either, and, at its best, it can
be beautifully buoyant. To the extent that the poet's love
energizes or sacramentalizes his vision, to just that extent is
the poet able to fulfill the true poet's need—and it is a religious need—to see the height and depth and breadth of
things. Such is the poetry of transcendence, and such is the
quality of the poems that I have chosen for this book.

                                        SAMUEL HAZO

BROTHER ANTONINUS

GOD GERMED IN RAW GRANITE

God germed in raw granite, source-glimpsed in stone?
Or imaged out in the black-flamed
Onyx-open line, smoldered in the tortured
Free-flow of lava, the igneous
Instant of conception? As maiden-form
Swells in the heaviness of wold, sleeps
Rumped and wanton-bulged in the boulder's
Bulk, is shaped in tree-forms everywhere
As any may see; dropped logs, say, or those crotched
Trunks pronged like a reckless nymph
Head-plunged into the earth—so Godhood
Wakes under water, shape-lurked, or grave and somber,
Where sea falls, mocks through flung foam . . .

Ghost!
Can this be?   Breather of elemental truths,
She stirs, she coaxes! Out of my heart's howk,
Out of my soul's wild wrath
I make oath! In my emptiness
These arms gall for her, bride's mouth,
Spent-breathed in laughter, or that night's
First unblushing revealment, the flexed
Probity of the flesh, the hymen-hilted troth,
We closed, we clung on it, the stroked
And clangorous rapture!

I am dazed.
Is this she? Woman within!
Can this be? Do we, His images, float
Time-spun on that vaster drag
His timelessness evokes?
In the blind heart's when we,
Well-wedded merge, by Him
Twained into one and solved there,

17

Are these still three? Are three
So oned, in the full-forthing
(Heart's reft, the spirit's great
Unreckonable grope, and God's
Devouring splendor in the stroke) are we—
This all, this utterness, this terrible
Total truth—indubitably He?

DANIEL BERRIGAN, S.J.

THE CRUCIFIX

(for an eighty-sixth birthday)

I

I remember today a Quebec roadside, the crucifix
raised crude as life among farming people,
its shadow creeping, dawn and twilight, over their lives.
Among wains, haycocks and men it moved like a savior.

So old, so scored by their winters, it had been staked out
perhaps by a band of ruffians on first Good Friday.
The way it endured, time would have bruised his fist in
striking it.

What time had done, breaking the bones at knee and wrist,
washing the features blank as quarry stone,
turning the legs to spindles, stealing the eyes

was only to plant forever its own great gesture
deeper in furrow, heave it high above rooftops.

Where time had done his clumsy worst, cracking its heart,
hollowing its breast inexorably,—he opened this Burning-glass
to hold the huge landscape: crops, houses and men, in Its fire.

II

He was irremovably there, nailing down the landscape,
more permanent than any mountain time could bring down
or frost alter face of. He could not be turned aside
from his profound millennial prayer: not by birds
moved wonderfully to song on that cruel bough:
not by sun, standing compassionately at right hand or left.

Let weathers tighten or loosen his nails: he was vowed to
stand.

19

Northstar took rise from his eyes, learned constancy of him.
Let cloudburst break like judgment, sending workmen home-
ward
whipping their teams from field, down the rutted road to barn

still his body took punishment like a mainsail
bearing the heaving world onward to the Father.

And men knew nightlong: in the clear lovely morning he will
be there,
not to be pulled down from landscape, never from his people's
hearts.

LONELINESS. (Joseph speaks)

To be a part of things, to be apart from them:

Every spring I dunged and pruned the peach row
on south hillside: every autumn, like a stranger
took down the fruit whose face met my surprise
with its odor and wet, only half remembered or deserved.

Or watched from a doorway, artisans
summoning out of a dumb stick some form of beauty,
the fine grain emerging along hand or arm like a pulse,
every sigh of the blade saying, *I did not do that*.

Or parleyed with old trees in my yard
that shift painfully in the noon wind, heads together
nodding a memory awake. I did not lead them there:
they were already old when my father slept
a boy's hour, a drowsy noon in their shade.

I had even less to do with the stars
that having led her to me, bring her still face to me
evening and dawn, making of evening and dawn
one tranquil ecstasy.
                    Blade, hoe, manhood—
what have my tools to do with What wakes in her?

SAINT ANN
(who bore a daughter in late life)

Hand that folded and laid aside my fabric
as it pleased Him

                    when it pleased Him,
                    shook me out,
billowed and filled me like a silken tent
pegged in mid-desert.

                    He struck eventual waters
from this worn stone.

                    A voice, I come
shaking the women up at dawn, barefoot
through burning snow, and shouting *manna manna*

ELIZABETH BISHOP

ROOSTERS

At four o'clock
in the gun-metal blue dark
we hear the first crow of the first cock

just below
the gun-metal blue window
and immediately there is an echo

off in the distance,
then one from the back-yard fence,
then one, with horrible insistence,

grates like a wet match
from the broccoli patch,
flares, and all over town begins to catch.

Cries galore
come from the water-closet door,
from the dropping-plastered henhouse floor,

where in the blue blur
their rustling wives admire,
the roosters brace their cruel feet and glare

with stupid eyes
while from their beaks there rise
the uncontrolled, traditional cries.

Deep from protruding chests
in green-gold medàls dressed,
planned to command and terrorize the rest,

the many wives
who lead hens' lives
of being courted and despised;

deep from raw throats
a senseless order floats
all over town. A rooster gloats

over our beds
from rusty iron sheds
and fences made from old bedsteads,

over our churches
where the tin rooster perches,
over our little wooden northern houses,

making sallies
from all the muddy alleys,
marking out maps like Rand McNally's:

glass headed pins,
oil-golds and copper greens,
anthracite blues, alizarins,

each one an active
displacement in perspective;
each screaming, "This is where I live!"

Each screaming
"Get up! Stop dreaming!"
Roosters, what are you projecting?

You, whom the Greeks elected
to shoot at on a post, who struggled
when sacrificed, you whom they labeled

"Very combative . . ."
what right have you to give
commands and tell us how to live,

cry "Here!" and "Here!"
and wake us here where are
unwanted love, conceit and war?

The crown of red
set on your little head
is charged with all your fighting blood.

Yes, that excrescence
makes a most virile presence,
plus all that vulgar beauty of irridescence.

Now in mid-air
by twos they fight each other.
Down comes a first flame-feather,

and one is flying,
with raging heroism defying
even the sensation of dying.

And one has fallen,
but still above the town
his torn-out, bloodied feathers drift down;

and what he sung
no matter. He is flung
on the gray ash-heap, lies in dung

with his dead wives
with open, bloody eyes,
while those metallic feathers oxidize.

St. Peter's sin
was worse than that of Magdalen
whose sin was of the flesh alone;

of spirit, Peter's,
falling, beneath the flares,
among the "servants and officers."

Old holy sculpture
could set it all together
in one small scene, past and future:

Christ stands amazed,
Peter, two fingers raised
to surprised lips, both as if dazed.

But in between
a little cock is seen
carved on a dim column in the travertine.

explained by *gallus canit;*
flet Petrus underneath it.
There is inescapable hope, the pivot;

yes, and there Peter's tears
run down our chanticleer's
sides and gem his spurs.

Tear-encrusted thick
as a medieval relic
he waits. Poor Peter, heart-sick,

still cannot guess
those cock-a-doodles yet might bless,
his dreadful rooster come to mean forgiveness.

a new weathervane
on basilica and barn,
and that outside the Lateran

there would always be
a bronze cock on a porphyry
pillar so the people and the Pope might see

that even the Prince
of the Apostles long since
had been forgiven, and to convince

all the assembly
that "Deny deny deny,"
is not all the roosters cry.

In the morning
a low light is floating
in the backyard, and gilding

from underneath
the broccoli, leaf by leaf;
how could the night have come to grief?

gilding the tiny
floating swallow's belly
and lines of pink cloud in the sky,

the day's preamble
like wandering lines in marble.
The cocks are now almost inaudible.

The sun climbs in,
following "to see the end,"
faithful as enemy, or friend.

THE PRODIGAL

The brown enormous odor he lived by
was too close, with its breathing and thick hair.
for him to judge. The floor was rotten; the sty
was plastered halfway up with glass-smooth dung.
Light-lashed, self-righteous, above moving snouts.
the pigs' eyes followed him, a cheerful stare—
even to the sow that always ate her young—
till, sickening, he leaned to scratch her head.
But sometimes mornings after drinking bouts
(he hid the pints behind a two-by-four),
the sunrise glazed the barnyard mud with red;
the burning puddles seemed to reassure.
And then he thought he almost might endure
his exile yet another year or more.

But evenings the first star came to warn.
The farmer whom he worked for came at dark
to shut the cows and horses in the barn
beneath their overhanging clouds of hay,
with pitchforks, faint forked lightnings, catching light,
safe and companionable as in the Ark.
The pigs stuck out their little feet and snored.
The lantern—like the sun, going away—
laid on the mud a pacing aureole.
Carrying a bucket along a slimy board,
he felt the bats' uncertain staggering flight,
his shuddering insights, beyond his control,
touching him. But it took him a long time
finally to make his mind up to go home.

CARL BODE

PERSONAL LETTER TO THE EPHESIANS

Breaking through the sandy soil
The bony finger rises, then
Grows into an arm;
And all can see the bony mouth
Fixed on the word Alarm.

But none can taste the salt
Of terror, not having died
Themselves, not having known
The smothering grave nor
The crushing weight of stone.

But these bones of John the Baptist
Will flower into flesh
And he will walk anointed
With oils of fragrant hawthorn,
Bright bleeding-heart and pointed

Valentine. There is no life
Without a death, perhaps no
Peace without a terror.
Beware of crying out the truth
Unless, O men of Ephesus,
You also speak in error.

THE GOOD EARTH

He lies who says there are no saints on earth—
Lies or is blind or ignorant as a beast.
But who proclaims the cross? As best
The scrawny bigot
Rooting the red clay for his saving.

The rushing April rain washes over the red
Clay hills and floods all greenery
Away, leaving the ugly farms
Sterile and the one
Dirty town naked with animals.

Yet there are a few saints. I even know
More than one. But most of us: sows
Defending—or devouring—what we
Beget; malicious hens;
Dogs mounting
Each other at the street corner;

Celebrating spring on red mud farms or muddy
Streets, Lord Jesus, what is there,
What can you see in most of us
To make us
Worth the saving?

PHILIP BOOTH

LETTER FROM A DISTANT LAND

> I, on my side, require of every writer, first
> or last, a simple and sincere account of his own
> life . . . some such account as he would send to
> his kindred from a distant land; for if he has
> lived sincerely, it must have been in a distant
> land to me.
>
> —Thoreau. *Walden*

Henry, my distant kin,
                    I live halfway.
halfway between an airfield and your pond.
halfway within the house I moved to buy
by borrowing. On transcendental ground,
come south from colder hills and early dusk.
we claim two acres of uneven land.
Alone now, sitting at my birch-plank desk,
I see an acre out these wide new windows:
my wife cuts brush, two small girls both risk
a foot in appletrees. Across the meadows.
the alder swamp, an ash grove not yet green.
a pair of jets outrace their double shadows.
We do not look up. A grosbeak in the pine
pecks under wing, the shy hen pheasant leaves
her nibbled sumac for our scattered grain.
With rabbits, too, we share uncertain lives;
not quiet or desperate, we measure man
by how he lives and what he most believes.
I am half teacher, half-week chopping blow-down
for our fire. half-time professing words
to warm new minds with what my heart has known.
My classes are good failures. Afterwards.
I change clothes, moult my partial self,
and walk completed through the open woods.
Behind the grillwork branches where I half
confess. the chapel that I most attend
is choired by migratory birds; I loaf

30

within the absolution of the wind.
My thought is swiftest when my feet are slow,
but far abroad I own a spendthrift mind.
My Spanish grandfather, a tall man, knew
his knighthood from a book. So, pastoral
beside a fire, do I come slowly to know
you, odd Uncle of my wakeful, still,
and secret dawns. My least experiments
with seed, like yours with a dried apple, fail:
the weeds, slugs, borers, grow as dense
as crows. I own a herd dog, but no sheep;
my cultivation is, like learning, chance.
Slack puritan I am, I let my garden shape
itself with skunks. I am halfway, I tell you;
there are midnights when I do not sleep.

The quick night-fighters' sudden thunder shakes
this house awake. I know no metaphor
for them except to say they are great sharks
with silver fins that plane the ocean air.
Propelled by jets of flame fired through their vents,
they school a noisy mile Northeast of here,
guided by blind pilots, and by governments.
A war ago, I flew myself. Now, bound
to these two acres, I owe the several debts
a lonely conscience knows. I love this land
by the salt sweat it costs to own it whole.
My birthday was a bucksaw. I still defend
the new growth with an ax; the trees I fell
need cutting to let the hardwood grow. I chop
at the lush swamp, hack down the summer jungle
rich with flies. You know how fires earned chip
by chip are warmest. Still, you could not guess
the shapes of proved destruction. Chain saws rape
a virgin stand to stumps. Raw foremen boss
more horsepower in a fleet of airfield trucks
than Concord ever stabled. Machines as murderous
as mad bulls gore the land. Where stacked cornshocks
stood last fall, an orange oil tank flaws
the spring; girders bloom with concrete blocks.

So far, your Concord has seen four more wars.
Vegetables are high. The streets are filled
with tourists. Cheap people in expensive cars
patrol the Sunday roads. An acre sold
in 1849 sells now two hundred times
the price. Lexington is houses sprawled
on desert-dusty streets with fertile names.
The arrogant inherit lust. Everywhere,
thick rows of sportsmen fish polluted streams.
or hunt the posted woods of their own fear.
Overhead, the tight-paired jets write
cryptic warnings on the thin blue air.

Too close to earth to show to those who scan
the sky for enemy, I walked last week
beyond the impulse caught on any radar screen.
In windworn March, halfway to dawn, I woke
to feel the growing day: the wind light North-
north-west, the morning luminous, a streak
of cloud between the sunward-turning earth
and yesterday's last stars. A rebel drummer
called me like the crows. The cross-lots path
I walked was wet with melting frost, a rumor
of frogs thawed the swamp, and toward town
I heard the hard first whack of a hammer.
A casual pilgrim to the phoebe's tune,
I whistled down the distant land where you
(this same month's end) tramped out to cut white pine
with Alcott's borrowed ax. Your Walden, now.
is still half yours: a summer swimmer's beach
corrupts the eastern bank, the sun-up view,
but you, who would be saint in a formal church.
are honored still on the farther shores, preserved
in the commonwealth of hemlock, elm, and birch.
Your hut is marked by stone, the pond was saved
by taxes for a public park. Emerson's
strict laws of compensation have reserved
a parking space for Sunday lovers: beer cans
drift where you knelt soberly to drink,

and small boys smoke like truant puritans.
Such is August on the swimmers' bank,
but not my sharp March dawn. Between ice-out
and spring, I walk in time to hear the honk
of two stray geese, the song of a white-throat
soloing after his mate in your celibate woods.
It is the same, I tell you. Shadowy trout
rise like the swift perfection of your words,
the backyard journal of your human praise
is proved in the red oaks' blood-dark buds.
I like to think how animals would freeze
to see your stick, your crooked genius, poke
the leafy underbrush; until you froze
yourself, and all the thicket woodcock, duck,
and small scared beasts of Walden's shore
turned curious. Here, between the dark
and sudden milktrain day, halfway from fear,
halfway to spring, I say these natural names
to honor you as poet of the turning year.
Beside the ministry of waves, the times
of men are seasons, windfall seeds that spill
toward fruit: the perfect globe or wormy shames
of Adam. All poets climb back Eden's hill
within their own backyard. Woods and pond
were your recovery of the crop that's possible,
a harvest of good words grown from the land
that brings the whole world home. I cultivate
a different orchard, pruning under the sound
of probable war. The day's first silver jet
reflects first sunlight where I turn away
from Walden, turn, stop, look back, and start
again. Up the bank, I cross the highway
where a skunk got lost in headlights: traffic-
flat, his flowering intestines lie halfway
in sun. This new March day is sweetened thick
with death. But when was any season less?
You felt the cold fall snap of John Brown's neck,
owned a winter conscience, smelled slavery's grass-
fire torch the long dry land to civil war,
from Bull Run to Savannah to the Wilderness.

I tell you, Henry, distant as we are,
the good, the brave, are no more a majority
than when you walked this far spring shore.
Man, by his human nature, is not free,
but where his wildness is alive to swamp
and hill, he learns to live most naturally.
Still, a saunterer must make his camp
in strange unholy lands, begging alms
and passage for belief. I take no stump
except for liberty to listen to the elms,
to walk the cold wood, to sleep on bedrock
thought, and to say my winter psalms.
A century from where your wisdom struck
its temporary camp, I cross the middleground
toward truth. At home beneath both oak
and jet, praising what I halfway understand,
I walk this good March morning out
to say my strange love in a distant land.

EDGAR BOWERS

THE VIRGIN MARY

The hovering and huge, dark, formless sway
That nature moves by laws we contemplate
We name for lack of name as order, fate,
God, principle, or primum mobile.
But in that graven image, word made wood
By skillful faith of him to whom she was
Eternal nature, first and final cause,
The form of knowledge knowledge understood
Bound human thought against the dark we find.
And body took the image of the mind
To shape in chaos a congruent form
Of will and matter, equal, side by side.
Upon the act of faith, within the norm
Of carnal being, blind and glorified.

JOHN MALCOLM BRINNIN

BEFORE THERE WAS NO REASON IN THE WORLD

Before there was no reason in the world
As now there is
I was the bough bent easy by a bird
I was the vague blue-grazing flock
The sleeping and invisible

Before there was no reason in the world
As now there is
The course of waters was my only course
My repetitious oceans' sough and swell
My reasons pleasurable

Before there was no reason in the world
As now there is
To measure time from sleep I rose to sleep
To measure space I pastured on surprise
O meadows of resemblances

Before there was no reason in the world
As now there is
I was the grove on whose mosaic floors
The seeds of otherwise were spent
My gods had many arms

I was the Caesar of unmarshalled grass
Faustus in the branches
My first ambitions were my sorrows long
Before there was no reason in the world
As now there is

JOHN CIARDI

ELEGY FOR SANDRO

Read down into the dead and close
tiers of the lying sand, soil, grass—
the root-sided, landsliding, unraisable
dawn and dark of the pit—
my stupid cousin, the missing
scholar of all, father of nothing, and boxer
who never won a fight,
lies dumb to the tears of women.

From the womb that stirred in dreams and soft
from dream dark coiled awake the son
of the man-touched, man-giving, and oh unholdable
sweet and milk of the flesh;
to dissolution and the swaying
censer like a pendulum under the timing sky;
the woman who was gifted
gives back her barren son.

He was the oaf of her litter, but not less
love's nor death's. Her better sons—
the un-needing, Sunday-visiting, check-writing
first felt of her blood—
stay her faint at the trembling sill;
but he was the last to need her and first
most gone from all morning
she held to her breasts' greatness.

While this one lived she had a child and was
mother to man. Childless, she sees him down
the flower-spilled, sand-back, and infolding ways
into the blood-black deep past
tears and time to the stone-stopped heart.
A pebble rattles there. The skirted priest
runs out of saints and ends. Her big sons turn her
back to the world where now she is their child.

J. V. CUNNINGHAM

THE WANDERING SCHOLAR'S PRAYER
TO ST. CATHERINE OF EGYPT

Past ruined cities down the grass.
Past wayside smokers in the shade.
Clicking their heels the fruit cars pass
Old stations where the night is stayed.

Curved on the racking wheel's retreat.
Sweet Catherine, rise from time to come!
Number in pain the fruit car fleet.
And throw confusion in the sum!

The vagrants smoke in solitude.
Sick of the spittle without cough.
Not unabsolved do they grow rude.
Dying with Swift in idiot froth.

From revery, sweet saint, forfend
These ravelled faces of the park!
When questing cars at twilight's end
Cozen the eyes with chilling dark.

Save them from memory of the light.
The circuit of the orient sun
Wheeling loud silence through the night
Like headlamps where the twin rails run.

DONALD F. DRUMMOND

EPITAPH BELOW A CRUCIFIX

Slight is the leaf; slender the tree:
Hew out the cross, and let it be.
Death of the tree, wither of leaf:
Now is the season of my grief.

Now, of the time the bud at first
Swelled of itself, and swelling, burst,
Let me recall as I raise this cross,
How burst of bud and of leaf was loss.

Loss of the hard green form and sheath,
Of the tension building underneath,
Of the fire it nurtured and once contained:
Mark how the strong brown trunk is stained.

At the burst of a red bud secretly
Nurtured by gall, the ecstasy
Lost in a form I cannot know
Except that dying made it so.

ALAN DUGAN

HOLIDAY

After hundreds of years of common sense
action appeared at the corners of all eyes:
lights appeared at night, and sounds of war
whammed from the desert back of town.

At first only the outlying saints saw them,
but later they strolled through the streets:
bat-faced devils walking arm in arm
with blond white angels in a tourists' truce.

It was then that Natural Law was repealed
and a public virgin wept that it was she
to whom a fiend or angel had appeared
announcing an unearthly rape of sorts
and the arrival of a difficult child.

RICHARD EBERHART

THE HORSE CHESTNUT TREE

Boys in sporadic but tenacious droves
Come with sticks, as certainly as Autumn,
To assault the great horse chestnut tree.

There is a law governs their lawlessness.
Desire is in them for a shining amulet
And the best are those that are highest up.

They will not pick them easily from the ground.
With shrill arms they fling to the higher branches,
To hurry the work of nature for their pleasure.

I have seen them trooping down the street
Their pockets stuffed with chestnuts shucked, unshucked.
It is only evening keeps them from their wish.

Sometimes I run out in a kind of rage
To chase the boys away: I catch an arm,
Maybe, and laugh to think of being the lawgiver.

I was once such a young sprout myself
And fingered in my pocket the prize and trophy.
But still I moralize upon the day

And see that we, outlaws on God's property,
Fling out imagination beyond the skies
Wishing a tangible good from the unknown.

And likewise death will drive us from the scene
With the great flowering world unbroken yet,
Which we held in idea, a little handful.

THE FURY OF AERIAL BOMBARDMENT

You would think the fury of aerial bombardment
Would rouse God to relent; the infinite spaces
Are still silent. He looks on shock-pried faces.
History, even, does not know what is meant.

You would feel that after so many centuries
God would give man to repent; yet he can kill
As Cain could, but with multitudinous will,
No farther advanced than in his ancient furies.

Was man made stupid to see his own stupidity?
Is God by definition indifferent, beyond us all?
Is the eternal truth man's fighting soul
Wherein the Beast ravens in its own avidity?

Of Van Wettering I speak, and Averill,
Names on a list, whose faces I do not recall
But they are gone to early death, who late in school
Distinguished the belt feed lever from the belt holding pawl.

JOHN FANDEL

GRAVEYARD

A quietness defined by stone
Dating the attributes of bone
Lying in state for empty eyes
Of dust and easter morning skies.

The grass breathes greenly low upon
The stone on bone where breath is gone
That shaped the dust into the sun
With shadow, one for everyone.

To see the solemn gravities
From where I stand and count the sum
Between the worn biographies
Of birth and death, makes martyrdom

A gravity, this quiet pass
Between to be and was. The grass
Upon the stone décor of death
Means life, the ligaments of breath.

Means Life. I stand outside the fence
That guards like bayonets the tense
And ordered quietudes of death,
And breathe my breath, and hold my breath.

NORMA FARBER

TREE OF BLAME

O tree fulfilled with blame, o tree of burden
and bliss and fiery juice and taste of sin
like fruit, o prominent plant, o stem of pain,
o apple-bleeding branch in a myth of garden
where jungle festered and the fang was hidden
and God dissembled to his creature man,
and truth spoke from a snake; o tree made plain
by wrath: see, before the bole is rotten
you shall connive again against a man,
and sweat with sap exacted from his eyes.
blaze by his anguish, and be bled into
in wounds like his through the solicitu-
dinous night, and be recited later o less
and less a tree, and more and more a cross.

WHILE EVE

How like a man that earliest Adam blamed
Eve in a grove, as if he manly ate
evil for chivalry's sake, as if that meat
dried up his mouth with dread. How he disclaimed
the pulp a petal on his tongue, the inflamed
fruit-skin a sunrise glutting in his throat.
How he contemned the trespass now too late.
and the reptile writhing and the woman becalmed;
while Eve: while downcast Eve upheld the snake
for its true serpenthood, upheld the tree
laden with ache, upheld the ache, and the sky
clouded with dark Jehovah. And her nak-
edness and self alone did not uphold,
but covered up her shame, and still was cold.

ISABELLA GARDNER

TIMEO

Dear God (safe ambiguity)
If I address you faithlessly
The fear of heaven devils me.
Could I be sure of purgatory
Sure I could praise and not adore thee
I might a tepid faith embrace.
But I am terrified of grace.
Gethsemane is any place.

COCK A' HOOP

How struts my love my cavalier
How crows he like a chanticleer
How softly I am spurred my dear;
Our bed is feathered with desire
And this yard safe from fox and fire.
But spurless on the dunghill, dead,
The soldier's blood is rooster red,
His seed is spent and no hen fed.
Alas no chick of this sweet cock
Will speak for Christ at dawn o'clock.

45

SUZANNE GROSS

DIRGE FOR A NEW MEXICAN PRELATE

Now, now, in my body and cries,
I will command, or beg them, so:
that for no pride and no fear's sake
they would paint him as if he lives
and will get up again to work.

It is a love's beggary, this
crying at their Georgian doors:
let his body be, and be flesh,
without a mockery of rouge
and powder for an evil shame.

Let him lie dead and his gold bones
rest. And his flesh sunder and say
to terror and unloving lies
how he died in his need's desire,
soon, like the bright and virgin bee

used up for his honey riches,
shattered on the wing. Dare any
trick his love to hide his broken eyes,
plump out his fallen cheeks with wax,
or redden his wounded shy mouth?

Princes' kisses honor his face,
more kind than their coral and rose.
Let him sleep naked in the earth,
in the roots of the red mountains,
and the precious clays lie close and wait.

MONTOYA IN EXILE

In Peña Blanca someone,
perhaps the grandfather of a cousin,
still had oxen when I was small. Two white
oxen in a yoke of yellow wood, standing to breathe
at the end of a red field, let me touch
their faces, and bunch their dewlaps in my fist.
They smelled like Bethlehem.

Peña Blanca's two bronze bells
boomed
me out of bed in darkness. And I ran
across the dry arroyo and up the hard packed street
to church, to serve the Mass. Shameless I ate my God
and when I stepped out on the street again
it was day.

In Peña Blanca the boy named me
lay face up in bed, naked, and listened
to young men in the street pour music
off their hands, marvelous as water
running in the sun.
It doesn't matter any more
that I couldn't follow what they sang.
When I found the heart of the man named me,
it was already broken.

When I lived in Peña Blanca,
horses my aunts' husbands harnessed to harrow
were horses. Horses I rode
were the blue wind and thunder. Sundays,
after Mass and meal, we rode out all together,
brothers and cousins and friends, to the sound
that we hide in our hearts: hoofs beating
the sand and the jingling of bridles.
I rode on the mesas alone. Alone,
without English or shoes or shame,
I sat my holy horse on the bloody rocks,
looking to the Jemez mountains west,

Sandía southeast, southwest Ladrones,
and Sangre de Cristo at my back. The world
my fathers and their fathers' fathers named
lay at the feet of my horse. My own blood
sang to me in drops of fire, my bones were bugles.

My father moved us
all to Albuquerque
to find a better life.

                 In Albuquerque then,
under rainbows of glass, shamed, I ate
the windfallen fruit of the tree, the smiling worm
and all.

                 And my eyes
were opened. Now I see
the angel of the unborn son
armed in the arroyo, armed upon the rocks
and on the road to Cochití. Armed
in my breast he folds me in his wings
of doubled fires and whirls his flaming sword
through my father's falling hair,
through many women's thighs,
through airplanes and altars
of my mother's sighs. He spins his burning
promise in the spun bull's blood.

DONALD HALL

CHRISTMAS EVE IN WHITNEYVILLE

To My Father

December, and the closing of the year;
The momentary carolers complete
Their Christmas Eves, and quickly disappear
Into their houses on each lighted street.

Each car is put away in each garage;
Each husband home from work, to celebrate,
Has closed his house around him like a cage,
And wedged the tree until the tree stood straight.

Tonight you lie in Whitneyville again,
Near where you lived, and near the woods or farms
Which Eli Whitney settled with the men
Who worked at mass-producing firearms.

The main-street, which was nothing after all
Except a school, a stable, and two stores,
Was improvised and individual,
Picking its way alone, until the wars.

Now Whitneyville is like the other places.
Ranch-houses stretching flat beyond the square,
Same stores and movie, same composite faces
Speaking the language of the public air.

Old houses of brown shingle still surround
This churchyard where you wept when you were ten
And helped to set a coffin in the ground.
You left your friend from school behind you then.

Now you are back, a man of fifty-two.
Talk to the boy. Tell him about the years
When Whitneyville quadrupled, and how you
And all his friends went on to make careers,

Had cars as long as hayricks, boarded planes
For Rome and Paris where the pace was slow,
And took the time to think how yearly gains,
Profit and volume made the business grow.

"The things you had to miss," you said last week,
"Or thought you had to, take your breath away."
You propped yourself on pillows, where your cheek
Was hollow, stubbled lightly with new gray.

This love is jail; another sets us free.
Tonight the houses and their noise distort
The thin rewards of solidarity.
The houses lean together for support.

The noises fail. Now lights go on upstairs.
The men and women are undressing now
To go to sleep. They put their clothes on chairs
To take them up again. I think of how.

Across America, when midnight comes,
They lie together and are quieted,
To sleep as children sleep, who suck their thumbs,
Cramped in the narrow rumple of each bed.

They will not have unpleasant thoughts tonight.
They make their houses jails, and they will take
No risk of freedom for the appetite,
Or knowledge of it, when they are awake.

The lights go out and it is Christmas Day.
The stones are white, the grass is black and deep;
I will go back and leave you here to stay,
While the dark houses harden into sleep.

SARA HENDERSON HAY

NIGHT

Now to the moon's cold face
This side of the planet swings;
And, for a little space,
Disarmed in sleep they lie,
The savage and the brawling and the sly,
All enmity put by.
Mute as a stone those tongues
That all day long shouted or bragged or whined,
The hard, the bleared, the furtive eyes are blind.
The claw-curved hands fall open to relinquish
Whatever it is they hold
Of outraged honor or of charm-struck gold;
The lecherous and the traitorous and the bold
All, all, this fabulous innocency put on—
And who, by their soft breathing, could distinguish
The leapard from the fawn?

STONES

I like these bones of earth; the craggy shoulders
Of mountains thrust against the curve of sky;
The wrinkled skeleton outlines that the eye
Sees from a plane; and myriad shapes of boulders
By the enormous push of glaciers rounded;
Square-cut domestic stones, and granite ridges
In icy windswept solitude; the ledges
On sunny hills, and those by dark seas pounded.

Rocks high and steadfast; stones which may be turned,
Pebbles that, fitted to the sling or hand,
Can slay Philistines; shale with mica spangles,
Flint, and a certain stone which, men have learned,
Used as a pillow in a weary land
Starts in the cradled head a dream of angels.

SAMUEL HAZO

POSTSCRIPT TO MANY LETTERS
(For Robert George Hazo)

While other brothers meet and talk like foes
or strangers or alumni—hostile, cool
or banal—brotherhood is still our binding.
Somehow we have survived disintegration
since the quiet, Pittsburgh afternoons we walked
in rain bareheaded, scarfless, flaunting health,
the nights we smoked large, academic pipes
and read and talked philosophy, the years
of seminars and uniforms and trips
and letters postmarked Paris, Quantico,
Beirut, Jerusalem and San Francisco.

Nothing has changed or failed and still we have
"the same heroes and think the same men fools."
Our heroes still are individuals
resolved to face their private absolutes.
We see the fool in all who fail themselves
by choice and turn all promise cold with talk.
A Levantine who saw such folly done
two thousands years ago grew bored with life
and said only the unborn were worth blessing.
Not sticks, not any, not the sharpest stones
can bruise or break the unbegotten bones.

Yet, fools and our few heroes will persist.
We cannot bless the unborn flesh or wish
our times and cities back to countrysides
when wigwams coned into a twist of poles.
The future holds less answers than the past.
Salvation lies in choice, in attitude,
in faith that mocks glib gospelers who leave
the name of Jesus whitewashed on a cliff.
We still can shun what shames or shams the day
and keep as one our vigor in the bond
of blood where love is fierce but always fond.

TO MY MOTHER

Had you survived that August afternoon
of sedatives, you would be sixty-three,
and I would not be rummaging for words
to plot or rhyme what I would speak to you.

Tonight I found a diary you kept
in nineteen twenty-eight, and while I read
your script in English, Arabic and Greek,
I grudged those perished years and nearly wept

and cursed whatever god I often curse
because I never knew one day with you
or heard you sing or call me by my name.
I know you were a teacher and a nurse

and sang at all the summer festivals.
You made one scratched recording of a song
I often play when no one else is home,
but that is all I have to keep you real.

The rest exists in fragile photographs,
a sudden memoir in my father's eyes
and all the anecdotes of thirty years
remembered like a portrait torn in half

and torn in half again until a word
deciphered in a diary rejoins
these tatters in my mind to form your face
as magically as music overheard

can summon and assemble everything
about a day we thought forever past.
For one recovered second you are near.
I almost hear you call to me and sing

before the world recoils and returns . . .
I have no monument, my beautiful,
to offer you except these patterned lines.
They cannot sound the silentness that burns

and burns although I try to say at last
there lives beyond this treachery of words
your life in me anew and in that peace
where nothing is to come and nothing past.

THE ENCOUNTER

My purpose stays me when I walk,
and with its will it wills my steps
toward what sin or grace awaits.
I measure days by distances.

So have I paced the brickwork streets
at midnight in Annapolis,
fairways at Ligonier, Broadway
at crowd-time, cemetery lanes

to learn I am in each the same.
Steadfast to the back and fro of me,
the cities of man and God prevail.
A man of many steps and stops,

I walk a world that each man walks
to Emmaus, bewildered when
a saviour strides abreast and flees,
no footfall heard, no footprint seen.

BARBARA HOWES

A LULLABY

Landlocked, the child
Stirs, its curtained chamber
Blood-red in the blind dark, somnolent as amber;
Stirs: yet still the human
Alembic admits no change
But, tight in its leathern skin,
Climbs upon a landing
Where espaliered on the walls,
Doubled, the past dissolves
In two mirroring lanes. Yet all
Must come to birth. Can we
Reflecting the future, follow it there? Oh,
Landlocked, the child
Stirs, and will be born!

THE NUNS ASSIST AT CHILDBIRTH

Robed in dungeon black, in mourning
For themselves they pass, repace
The dark linoleum corridors
Of humid wards, sure in the grace

Of self-denial. Blown by duty,
Jet sails borne by a high wind,
Only the face and hands creep through
The shapeless clothing, to remind

One that a woman lives within
The wrappings of this strange cocoon.
Her hands reach from these veils of death
To harvest a child from the raw womb.

The metal scales of paradox
Tip here then there. What can the nun
Think of the butchery of birth,
Mastery of the flesh, this one

Vigorous mystery? Rude life
From the volcano rolls and pours,
Tragic, regenerate, wild. Sad
The unborn wait behind closed doors.

X. J. KENNEDY

ON A CHILD WHO
LIVED ONE MINUTE

Into a world where children shriek like suns
Sundered from other suns on their arrival,
She stared, and saw the waiting shape of evil,
But couldn't take its meaning in at once,
So fresh her understanding, and so fragile.

Her first breath drew a fragrance from the air
And put it back. However hard her agile
Heart danced, however full the surgeon's satchel
Of healing stuff, a blackness tiptoed in her
And snuffed the only candle of her castle.

O let us do away with elegiac
Drivel! Who can restore a thing so brittle,
So new in any jingle? Still I marvel
That, making light of mountainloads of logic,
So much could stay a moment in so little.

GALWAY KINNELL

TO CHRIST OUR LORD

The legs of the elk punctured the snow's crust
And wolves floated lightfooted on the land
Hunting Christmas elk living and frozen;
Inside snow melted in a basin, and a woman basted
A bird spread over coals by its wings and head.

Snow had sealed the windows; candles lit
The Christmas meal. The Christmas grace chilled
The cooked bird, being long-winded and the room cold.
During the words a boy thought, is it fitting
To eat this creature killed on the wing?

He had killed it himself, climbing out
Alone on snowshoes in the Christmas dawn,
The fallen snow swirling and the snowfall gone,
Heard its throat scream as the rifle shouted,
Watched it drop, and fished from the snow the dead.

He had not wanted to shoot. The sound
Of wings beating into the hushed air
Had stirred his love, and his fingers
Froze in his gloves, and he wondered,
Famishing, could he fire? Then he fired.

Now the grace praised his wicked act. At its end
The bird on the plate
Stared at his stricken appetite.
There had been nothing to do but surrender,
To kill and to eat; he ate as he had killed, with wonder.

At night on snowshoes on the drifting field
He wondered again, for whom had love stirred?
The stars glittered on the snow and nothing answered.
Then the Swan spread her wings, cross of the cold north,
The pattern and mirror of the acts of earth.

EASTER

We read of her death in the morning.
By the riverbank shreds of clothes and her purse.
Raped, robbed, weighted, drowned—
They conjecture the night-off of a virgin nurse.

To get to church you have to cross the river,
First breadwinner for the town, its wide
Mud-colored currents cleansing forever
The swill-making villages at its side.

The disinfected voice of the minister
For a moment is one of the clues,
But he is talking of nothing but Easter,
Dying so on the wood, He rose.

Some of us daydream of the morning news,
Some of us lament we rose at all,
A child beside me comforts her doll,
We are dying on the hard wood of the pews.

Death is everywhere, in the extensive
Sermon, the outcry of the inaudible
Prayer, the nickels, the dimes the poor give,
And outside, at last, in the gusts of April.

Upon the river, its Walden calm,
With wire hooks the little boats are fishing.
Those who can wait to get home
Line up, and lean on the railing, wishing.

Up through the mud can you see us
Waiting here for you, for hours,
Virgin lady, trapped or working loose,
Can you see our hats like a row of flowers?

Then we crown you with an Easter fire.
And if you do not rise before dinner
When the flower show must bow and retire,
Then drink well of the breadwinner,

And tomorrow when the brown water
Shall shove you senselessly on
Past smoking cities, works of disaster,
Kids playing ball, cows, unrealistic fishermen,

Toll bridges you slip under for free,
And you cast an eye from the brown lorry
Which floats your drenching flesh to sea,
Do not, moved by goodbyes, be altogether sorry

That the dream has ended. Turn
On the dream you lived through the unwavering gaze.
It is as you thought. The living burn.
In the floating days may you discover grace.

CAROLYN KIZER

A WIDOW IN WINTERTIME

Last night a baby gargled in the throes
Of a fatal spasm. My children are all grown
Past infant strangles; so, reassured, I knew
Some other baby perished in the snow.
But no. The cat was making love again.

Later, I went down and let her in.
She hung her tail, flagging from her sins.
Though she'd eaten, I forked out another dinner,
Being myself hungry all ways, and thin
From metaphysic famines she knows nothing of,

The feckless beast! Even so, resemblances
Were on my mind: female and feline, though
She preens herself from satisfaction, and does
Not mind lying even in snow. She is
Lofty and bedraggled, without need to choose.

As an ex-animal, I look fondly on
Her excesses and simplicities, and would not return
To them; taking no marks for what I have become,
Merely that my nine lives peal in my ears again
And again, ring in these austerities,

These arbitrary disciplines of mine,
Most of them trivial: like covering
The children on my way to bed, and trying
To live well enough alone, and not to dream
Of grappling in the snow, claws plunged in fur,

Or waken in a caterwaul of dying.

PHILIP LARKIN

CHURCH GOING

Once I am sure there's nothing going on
I step inside, letting the door thud shut.
Another church: matting, seats, and stone,
And little books; sprawlings of flowers, cut
For Sunday, brownish now; some brass and stuff
Up at the holy end; the small neat organ;
And a tense, musty, unignorable silence,
Brewed God knows how long. Hatless, I take off
My cycle-clips in awkward reverence,

Move forward, run my hand around the font.
From where I stand, the roof looks almost new—
Cleaned, or restored? Someone would know: I don't.
Mounting the lectern, I peruse a few
Hectoring large-scale verses, and pronounce
'Here endeth' much more loudly than I'd meant.
The echoes snigger briefly. Back at the door
I sign the book, donate an Irish sixpence,
Reflect the place was not worth stopping for.

Yet stop I did: in fact I often do,
And always end much at a loss like this,
Wondering what to look for; wondering, too,
When churches fall completely out of use
What we shall turn them into, if we shall keep
A few cathedrals chronically on show,
Their parchment, plate and pyx in locked cases,
And let the rest rent-free to rain and sheep.
Shall we avoid them as unlucky places?

Or, after dark, will dubious women come
To make their children touch a particular stone;
Pick simples for a cancer; or on some
Advised night see walking a dead one?
Power of some sort or other will go on
In games, in riddles, seemingly at random;

But superstition, like belief, must die,
And what remains when disbelief has gone?
Grass, weedy pavement, brambles, buttress, sky,

A shape less recognisable each week,
A purpose more obscure. I wonder who
Will be the last, the very last, to seek
This place for what it was; one of the crew
That tap and jot and know what rood-lofts were?
Some ruin-bibber, randy for antique,
Or Christmas-addict, counting on a whiff
Of gown-and-bands and organ-pipes and myrrh?
Or will he be my representative,

Bored, uninformed, knowing the ghostly silt
Dispersed, yet tending to this cross of ground
Through suburb scrub because it held unspilt
So long and equably what since is found
Only in separation—marriage, and birth,
And death, and thoughts of these—for whom was built
This special shell? For, though I've no idea
What this accoutred frowsty barn is worth,
It pleases me to stand in silence here;

A serious house on serious earth it is,
In whose blent air all our compulsions meet.
Are recognised, and robed as destinies.
And that much never can be obsolete,
Since someone will forever be surprising
A hunger in himself to be more serious.
And gravitating with it to this ground,
Which, he once heard, was proper to grow wise in,
If only that so many dead lie round.

DENISE LEVERTOV

THE JACOB'S LADDER

The stairway is not
a thing of gleaming strands
a radiant evanescence
for angels' feet that only glance in their tread, and need not
touch the stone.

It is of stone.
A rosy stone that takes
a glowing tone of softness
only because behind it the sky is a doubtful, a doubting
night gray.

A stairway of sharp
angles, solidly built.
One sees that the angels must spring
down from one step to the next, giving a little
lift of the wings:

and a man climbing
must scrape his knees, and bring
the grip of his hands into play. The cut stone
consoles his groping feet. Wings brush past him.
The poem ascends.

THE THREAD

Something is very gently,
invisibly, silently,
pulling at me—a thread
or net of threads
finer than cobweb and as
elastic. I haven't tried
the strength of it. No barbed hook

pierced and tore me. Was it
not long ago this thread
began to draw me? Or
way back? Was I
born with its knot about my
neck, a bridle? Not fear
but a stirring
of wonder makes me
catch my breath when I feel
the tug of it when I thought
it had loosened itself and gone.

PETER LEVI, S.J.

'WHAT IF THE WORLD WERE A HORRIBLE MAD FIT . . .'

What if the world were a horrible mad fit,
human reason sand, and God a mere unknown,
and no philosophies could temper it
to shivering flesh and nerve, breakable bone,
but the mind's vigour alone?

I would not choose to be masked in any defence
beyond the fight and heat of an animal,
and heart's power against heart's pretence;
some wild thing's ways, not copied or learnt at all,
some quiet of innocence.

IN MEMORIAM C.W.

He was a small, delightful, active man,
I was glad it was on Good Friday he died,
no one surely since the world began
had died so old and so innocent eyed.

Just as a frost in late autumn blights
some apple out of reach, withered and red,
and it seems the worst loss of those bad nights,
so it seemed when we heard he was dead.

All that suffering and age
were not so hard to understand,
but death in his ultimate lion rage
striking the cross out of the old man's hand—

and many a frost burns them in the grave,
old men's bodies worn to pure bone:
yet as if death were mocked somehow and could have
nothing in his hand but a skeleton,

or as if some spirit blew from the mouth like breath
and blood chills and pales, and bone sags,
or as if that tempestuous lion death
could be pacified with a few old bones and rags.

JOHN LOGAN

CYCLE FOR MOTHER CABRINI

1. A CHANCE VISIT TO HER BONES

I thank God Mother Cabrini's
Body is subject to laws
Of decay. To me it is
A disservice when flesh

Will not fall from bones
As God for His glory
Sometimes allows. I speak thus
For flesh is my failing:

That it shall fall is my
Salvation. That it shall not
Conquer is my blind hope.
That it shall rise again

Commanding, is my fear.
That it shall rise changed
Is my faith. I think
I can love this saint

Who built high schools
And whose bones I came upon
Today. I laugh a little
At the wax mask that smiles

Surely thru her box of glass:
Artificial faces cannot
Frighten one who remembers
No face is real for long.

Blessed Mother Cabrini
Lives here her saint's life
I said, she sees me all;
I only see her face

Mask, and see her habit
Given form by bones
Which carried about her flesh
Gone now. The bones will rise

To carry changed flesh
And I may walk I
Might walk with her!
Whom I seek to pray to

Some, and strain
To love. Moisten me
With dust from her bones.
I see their shape—help me

Love them help think of
Breast white doves that rise
Over earth-smelling fields
Their wings tremble for her

Birth, as I wait: mine
Is a dry waiting
Her mask stares, she
Stirs — ah

Her bones move *me!*

2. RECOLLECTION

i.

I found your bones that lay
Off the highschool hallway
And drummed them with my need;
They rang and rose and hurried

Me. I bought and set
Your picture in my wallet
And chose a cheap ring,
A piece of junk but something

Your sisters sell; to me
Its feel and pull heavy
On my fingerbone wore
In for a time, the terror

Of your delicate flesh, the scant
Weight within the fragrant
Bones that it seemed turned
To me as to the bright and the unburned

ii.

Blessed Mother I know
You met me once in Chicago
I didn't go there
To hunt for saints (or anywhere):

You bowed and smiled at me
Out of a film biography
I don't know why I went
Except perhaps for amusement

And rest; your skill is hid
Behind a sweet and lurid
Piety O queen
Of a Holy wood unseen —

Your eyes and art sent
A deep tiredness apparent
To me as an expected thing
But until I knew unsettling

Because of breathlessness
And hot and blood shocked duress
At my ribs, that sickened me,
And turned the colors of the city.

iii.

Long years Mother had gone
Before I met you in Tryon
Park although you knew me
At Chicago and eternally.

One time in New York again
Under the wicked regimen
Of grace, I thought to come
To your girls' kingdom

To the middy world of your tomb
By text, principal, and schoolroom.
You know I did not go;
I went another place though:

Can I say what you did
Those days I invalid
At church, ambiguous at its door
Was tried by my confessor;

Without lustre hair
Sprouts at arm's root bitter
Sediment upon the flesh dead
The nail slides from folded

Skin, so shall I be
Till Christ reafford the luxury
By which bodies sing
And souls have their breathing;

Sweet virgin it was you
That left the gay retinue
To cry me grace at its head
Till I like your bones was not dead.

iv.

Saint who overlaps
Our lives who knows the mishaps
Of our times the flaws
Of men no longer outlaws

Even; who knows our schools
Our stores our gods and business rules
Saw charts rise and fall
In your chromium hospital —

You helped shape our city
And the city in the sky:
Help me shape your beauty
In this scarred and remade eye.

3. MOTHER CABRINI CROSSES THE ANDES

In God's good time we reached the "Cumbre" which is the
topmost height that can be crossed in the neighborhood of
Aconcagua and here we remained some time.
                —St. Frances Xavier Cabrini, *Travels and Letters*

He has made my feet like the feet of harts; he has set me
upon high places.
                —Gradual from her Mass (Dec. 22)

i.

The tiny saint got the best mule
Though an opera singer was in the party,
And St. Joseph the muleteer was gentle
And helped a lot; providentially,

For the soundest beast leads
And she had never ridden and was jittery—
Tried to guide! Though she learned
Early to be passive to the sea.

Small and weightless as she was
She could have risen to the saddle
Or St. Joseph would have tossed her
Humbly, could she have put

Her foot into his hand
But she could not, ascending
Rather from upon a chair
And set off cowled in furs

Like a monk (her saving comment)
Or Xavier in the mountains of the orient.

ii.

And the air in the high Andes
Was thin and lucid as milk
Or fire, or as violets she sailed
In boats in Lombardy,

A child afraid of the water
But sick for the fire and milk
Of the sea's wake and for the souls
That flashed like fish

For the souls that love like milk
And like fire, for the spring soul
That bursts quiet as a violet
And swings upon its thin

Stem to flame at the sun.
Ridiculous as a nun.

iii.

Had she known the pressure
Here will bleed the skin
Or that the muleteers would be
Too busy to say the Rosary,
That she would fail to jump her mule a-

Cross a crevasse, would fall
Into St. Joseph's arms and
Faint in the snow bank that flanks
The rim (the heights of her cheeks
More pale more glowing than crystal
Vanishing on her habit — eyes

As they opened as soft as furs),
Or had she somehow discovered
She and Mother Chiara
Would spend the evening in a bar
Beside the pampas' edge: she

Would lead the pilgrimage again
Over the high Andes,
Forego the closed cabin
The turn around the horn, would climb
Would rest the party at the Cumbre
Again draw breath and for a moment again

Would turn away forever.

iv.

Air shivered in the Andes
As full of color as blood
Or bells, or ice the saboteurs
Left on Lytle Street
When angered by her sick and alien

They opened the mansion pipes;
What was this to her
Who dynamites hearts: rivets,
Quarries, shapes bricks, and built
In Chicago two hospitals
Besides the one they chilled awhile

And burned a little bit.
But they kicked the sisters out
Of Nicaragua—the schoolgirls no trash
These, necks blue as Andes
Snow thin as moons: and hair

Black as the bird-live valleys;
The saint was away on business —
New Orleans orphanage or the Villa
Or the novitiate at old Manresa
On the Hudson. (Or was it the hotel
In Seattle?) And there was trouble in France

Since the archbishop was on the Riviera,
And the priests turned her a cold
Parisian shoulder, but she moved in
At a gilt estate where the sisters
Had to put up sheets over the many mirrors.

Whether they went on their continents
Or ours the austere skirts
Were strangest brushing by the summer-house
In Rio the intemperate flower parts:
Though here the black was closest
To the holy red that flowed her into God.

In Chicago, upon her martyrdom.
She should have died in Lombardy
Safe from a saint's life and the traveler's
Malady that chilled her and brightened
Her gown, like a bell she jangled in her room
Where she rocked and, died, in a wicker chair.

v.

A good mule like god's will and the sea
Does not mind those who disagree
And bore her safely
So that, the stars at easy
Height again. the party
Rested.

But the pampas at night are a sky
Where masses alive and unknown
Are relieved by constellations of bone.

vi.

High cold keen the Cumbre air
As the light from the stone and shattering stars

But there is nowhere mountain air
So cold or keen or bright or
Thin as is Francesca's wrist
Humming hyaline
Along the risen limb.

REVIST TO THE ROOM OF A SAINT

The Shrine of St. Frances Xavier Cabrini
in Columbus Hospital, Chicago

Yesterday in Chicago for the moment
penitent, vigilant for her ancient feast,
I revisited her place of death
and found the blood of a saint she left
on the flesh colored mat
beside her tiny bed. What a doll she was.
Even her roll-top desk
with its postal scale seems small.
Her letter opener, paper clips, picture of The Pope,
blotter—and the folded, remarkable
eyeglass and ruler! I wanted to touch her gold-
topped pencil like my father's
but could only slip a finger
under the edge of the celluloid cover.
And there's a celluloid box
around the little, lifeless wicker chair
where she rocked
her self into the better air.
Beside the saint's spoon and cup
and her final clothes
are her ugly little shoes.
They stand without a step inside a glass case

skin cracked from twenty-seven trips over seas
and once over the angular, ivory
Andes. Her small, folded linens
have in them an aura of the gold mountain sun,
of fresh opened earth, of firs and rain,
the odors of The Virgin Queen.
A thing she wore, a kind of sleeveless shirt,
is feathered at the edges
as with lace, or with the brush
of her tiny bones as she moved,
habited and in her black
crochet-tipped hat or coif
over the earth, like an earth-bound little dove.
White doves wound above the field at her birth.
Now wine, gold and turquoise doves
rise surely for her death. Their tissue wings
thin and lucid as her light hands
make a light wind.
Let it breathe on my hidden face
as my beast
kneels a moment in this child's place.

ROBERT LOWELL

CHRISTMAS EVE UNDER HOOKER'S STATUE

Tonight a blackout. Twenty years ago
I hung my stocking on the tree, and hell's
Serpent entwined the apple in the toe
To sting the child with knowledge. Hooker's heels
Kicking at nothing in the shifting snow,
A cannon and a cairn of cannon balls
Rusting before the blackened Statehouse, know
How the long horn of plenty broke like glass
In Hooker's gauntlets. Once I came from Mass;

Now storm-clouds shelter Christmas, once again
Mars meets his fruitless star with open arms,
His heavy saber flashes with the rime,
The war-god's bronzed and empty forehead forms
Anonymous machinery from raw men;
The cannon on the Common cannot stun
The blundering butcher as he rides on Time —
The barrel clinks with holly. I am cold:
I ask for bread, my father gives me mould;

His stocking is full of stones. Santa in red
Is crowned with wizened berries. Man of war,
Where is the summer's garden? In its bed
The ancient speckled serpent will appear,
And black-eyed susan with her frizzled head.
When Chancellorsville mowed down the volunteer,
"All wars are boyish," Herman Melville said;
But we are old, our fields are running wild;
Till Christ again turn wanderer and child.

CHILDREN OF LIGHT

Our fathers wrung their bread from stocks and stones
And fenced their gardens with the Redman's bones;
Embarking from the Nether Land of Holland,
Pilgrims unhouseled by Geneva's night,
They planted here the Serpent's seeds to shock
And here the pivoting searchlights probe to shock
The riotous glass houses built on rock,
And candles gutter by an empty altar,
And light is where the landless blood of Cain
Is burning, burning the unburied grain.

THE HOLY INNOCENTS

Listen, the hay-bells tinkle as the cart
Wavers on rubber tires along the tar
And cindered ice below the burlap mill
And ale-wife run. The oxen drool and start
In wonder at the fenders of a car,
And blunder hugely up St. Peter's hill.
These are the undefiled by woman—their
Sorrow is not the sorrow of this world:
King Herod shrieking vengeance at the curled
Up knees of Jesus choking in the air,

A king of speechless clods and infants. Still
The world out-Herods Herod; and the year,
The nineteen-hundred forty-fifth of grace,
Lumbers with losses up the clinkered hill
Of our purgation; and the oxen near

The worn foundations of their resting-place,
The holy manger where their bed is corn
And holly torn for Christmas. If they die,
As Jesus, in the harness, who will mourn?
Lamb of the shepherds, Child, how still you lie.

WILLIAM H. MATCHETT

WATER OUZEL

for Dora Willson

Follow back from the gull's bright arc and the osprey's plunge,
Past the silent heron, erect in the tidal marsh,
Up the mighty river, rolling in mud. Branch off
At the sign of the kingfisher poised on a twisted snag.
Not deceived when the surface grows calm, keep on,
Past the placidity of ducks, the delusive pastoral dreams
Drawn down by the effortless swallows that drink on the wing.
With the wheat fields behind you, do not neglect to choose
At every juncture the clearest and coldest path.
Push through the reeds where the redwing sways,
Climb through the warnings of hidden jays,
Climb, climb the jostling, narrowing stream
Through aspen sunlight into the evergreen darkness
Where chattering crossbills scatter the shreds of cones.
Here at last at the brink of the furthest fall,
With the water dissolving to mist as it shatters the pool below,
Pause beneath timber-line springs and the melting snow.
Here, where the shadows are deep in the crystal air,
So near a myriad beginnings, after so long a journey,
Expecting at least a golden cockatoo
Or a screaming eagle with wings of flame,
Stifle your disappointment, observe
The burgher of all this beauty, the drab
Citizen of the headwaters; struggle to love
The ridiculous ouzel, perched on his slippery stone
Like an awkward, overblown catbird deprived of its tail.

Not for him the limitless soaring above the storm,
Or the surface-skimming, or swimming, or plunging in.
He walks. In the midst of the turbulence, bathed in spray,
From a rock without foothold into the lunging current
He descends a deliberate step at a time till, submerged,
He has walked from sight and hope. The stream

Drives on, dashes, splashes, drops over the edge,
Too swift for ice in midwinter, too cold
For life in midsummer, depositing any debris,
Leaf, twig or carcass, along the way,
Wedging them in behind rocks to rot,
Such as these not reaching the ocean.

Yet lo, the lost one emerges unharmed,
Hardly wet as he walks from the water.
Undisturbed by beauty or terror, pursuing
His own few needs with a nerveless will,
Nonchalant in the torrent, he bobs and nods
As though to acknowledge implicit applause.
This ceaseless tic, a trick of the muscles shared
With the solitary sandpiper, burlesqued
By the teeter-bob and the phoebe's tail,
Is not related to approbation. The dipper,
Denied the adventure of uncharted flight
Over vast waters to an unknown homeland, denied
Bodily beauty, slightly absurd and eccentric,
Will never attain acclaim as a popular hero.
No prize committee selects the clown
Whose only dangers are daily and domestic.

Yet he persists, and does not consider it persisting.
On a starless, sub-zero, northern night,
When all else has taken flight into sleep or the south,
He, on the edge of the stream, has been heard to repeat
The rippling notes of his song. which are clear and sweet.

SISTER M. MAURA, S.S.N.D.

TOURIST IN DANTE

Hell

He took the strata dome for comfort and
floodlights at night: Hell gate he saw and fire
outdid the myth of Hades, and he punned
the script—leave hope behind—for any bar.
The picture cards he bought he chose to gull
the rocker on the porch at home: the jaws
of Ugolino at the bishop's skull;
the Malebolge in flat color views;
another of the tidy giants' wall;
a mimic Hogarth of the hairy legs
of Lucifer; an abstract of the roll
and pitch of slothful clogged in mud like frogs.
And for himself a studio print he chose:
Democritus and Zeno called the wise.

Purgatory

He wearied of the terraces almost
immediately; disliked the hymnal rite,
the spiral tremor in the mountain crust
(no seismographic indication that
it could occur). The outworn shibboleth
of seven-three, the graven mountain side
he read, even the sculptured stone beneath
his feet, with clinical exactitude.
The too-bright traveling day revealed the catch,
the crowds, the tavern-like democracy.
A momentary thought of Malevich,
or Klee perhaps, soothed him as he saw
processional of candles, but light showed
the gryphon glorious. He caught the fraud.

Heaven

He dreaded most the gasp, the broken rune
of breath on breath. He clipped the traveler's mask
to mouth and nose but knew the oxygen
might fail. There was no one to ask. Star-discs
betrayed his sight. He thought he glimpsed a group
but it was all mercurial sound and light
honeycombing airy touchless slopes.
Somehow he was beyond the hurtling jet
of supersonic speed; he fought the rant
of choric peace, the native eloquent
propulsion toward an eye-unclouded point.
He could not wait to hail a taxi, flint
his lighter, suck a cigarette, get out
and to his room and drink a whiskey straight.

PHYLLIS McGINLEY

CONVERSATION IN AVILA

Teresa was God's familiar. She often spoke
To Him informally,
As if together they shared some heavenly joke.
Once, watching stormily
Her heart's ambitions wither to odds and ends,
With all to start anew,
She cried, "If this is the way You treat Your friends,
No wonder You have so few!"

There is no perfect record standing by
Of God's reply.

SIX NUNS IN THE SNOW

Beautifully, now, they walk among these new
petals the snow shook down—
identical figures, going two by two,
each in a black gown.

With what a placid tread, what definite,
calm impulse each proceeds,
two by two, black on bewildering white,
swinging her long beads;

an absolute six, taking their candid way
undazzled by this whiteness,
who have grown used to walking without dismay
amid incredible brightness.

SAMUEL MENASHE

O MANY NAMED BELOVED

O Many Named Beloved
Listen to my praise
Various as the seasons
Different as the days
All my treasons cease
When I see your face

THERE IS NO JERUSALEM BUT THIS

The shrine whose form within
My physical form is limned
Streams fire to my skin
And I, kilned one, chant
Canticles which flames scan
Through me shaped as I am

There is no Jerusalem but this
Breathed in flesh by shameless love
Built high upon the tides of blood
I believe the Prophets and Blake
And like David I bless myself
With all my might

I know many hills were holy once
But now in the level lands to live
Zion ground down must become marrow
Thus in my bones I'm the King's son
And through Death's domain I go
Making my own procession

WILLIAM MEREDITH

NOTRE DAME de CHARTRES

After God's house burned down, they found the shirt—
His mother Mary's shirt; it had not burned.
This was their kind of miracle: it spoke
Of continuing grace, if chastised. The Lord's mother
Would stay on; it was simply that the house
Had not pleased the holy visitor to France.

The town's good fortune must have stirred all France,
The preservation of that sacred shirt
Which had won battles for the royal house;
The citizens themselves whose town had burned
To the ground that night, thanked God's gracious mother
For the special favor that the flames bespoke.

The vast basilica they raised there spoke
Of a yearning that reached far beyond France,
A love that verged on heresy for the mother
Who had been brought to bed in this same shirt.
This is our miracle: the faith that burned
Bright and erroneous, and built that house.

I suppose there never will be such a house
Again, that has the power to make men speak
Of *an act of God,* where a dozen cities burned
Will not; to ask a pilgrimage to France
Of men and women who smile about the shirt
And doubt or know nothing of the mother.

The arbitrary doctrine of the Mother
Is no harder to believe than her great house
At Chartres, copied from heaven, to hold a shirt.
Stand at the transept when the delicate spokes
Of stone glow black against the sun of France:
It is as if the virgin's faith still burned.

Or as if the ancient glass itself still burned,
If you prefer that to the legend of God's mother.
Whatever it is, no splendor now in France
Puzzles the heart like the molten light in this house;
Probably no one who saw it ever spoke
Coarsely again of the medieval shirt.

Sancta Camisa, the blessed shirt of the Mother,
Because it had not burned, required a house
And spoke to the stone that slept in the groin of France.

A KOREAN WOMAN SEATED BY A WALL

Suffering has settled like a sly disguise
On her cheerful old face. If she dreams beyond
Rice and a roof, now toward the end of winter,
Is it of four sons gone, the cries she has heard,
A square farm in the south, soured by tents?
Some alien and untranslatable loss
Is a mask she smiles through at the weak sun
That is moving north to invade the city again.

A poet penetrates a dark disguise
After his own conception, little or large.
Crossing the scaleless asia of trouble
Where it seems no one could give himself away,
He gives himself away, he sets a scale.
Hunger and pain and death, the sorts of loss,
Dispute our comforts like peninsulas
Of no particular value, places to fight.
And what it is in suffering dismays us more:
The capriciousness with which it is dispensed
Or the unflinching way we see it borne?

She may be dreaming of her wedding gift;
A celadon bowl of a good dynasty
With cloud and heron cut in its green paste,
It sleeps in a hollow bed of pale blue silk.
The rice it bought was eaten the second winter.

And by what happier stove is it unwrapped
In the evening now and passed around like a meat,
Making a foliage in the firelight?

She shifts the crate she sits on as the March
Wind mounts from the sea. The sun moves down the sky
Perceptibly, like the hand of a public clock,
In increments of darkness though ablaze.
Ah, now she looks at me. We are unmasked
And exchange what roles we guess at for an instant.
The questions Who comes next and Why not me
Rage at and founder my philosophy.
Guilt beyond my error and a grace past her grief
Alter the coins I tender cowardly,
Shiver the porcelain fable to green shards.

JAMES MERRILL

ANGEL

Above my desk, whirring and self-important
(Though not much larger than a hummingbird)
In finely woven robes, school of Van Eyck,
Hovers an evidently angelic visitor.
He points one index finger out the window
At winter snatching to its heart,
To crystal vacancy, the misty
Exhalations of houses and of people running home
From the cold sun pounding on the sea;
While with the other hand
He indicates the piano
Where the Sarabande No. 1 lies open
At a passage I shall never master
But which has already, and effortlessly. mastered me.
He drops his jaw as if to say, or sing,
'Between the world God made
And this music of Satie,
Each glimpsed through veils, but whole,
Radiant and willed,
Demanding praise, demanding surrender,
How can you sit there with your notebook?
What do you think you are doing?
However he says nothing—wisely: I could mention
Flaws in God's world, or Satie's; and for that matter
How did he come by *his* taste for Satie?
Half to tease him, I turn back to my page,
Its phrases thus far clotted, unconnected.
The tiny angel shakes his head.
There is no smile on his round, hairless face.
He does not want even these few lines written.

THOMAS MERTON

FOR MY BROTHER
REPORTED MISSING IN ACTION, 1943

Sweet brother, if I do not sleep
My eyes are flowers for your tomb;
And if I cannot eat my bread,
My fasts shall live like willows where you died.
If in the heat I find no water for my thirst,
My thirst shall turn to springs for you, poor traveler.

Where, in what desolate and smoky country,
Lies your poor body, lost and dead?
And in what landscape of disaster
Has your unhappy spirit lost its road?

Come, in my labor find a resting place
And in my sorrows lay your head,
Or rather take my life and blood
And buy yourself a better bed—
Or take my breath and take my death
And buy yourself a better rest.

When all the men of war are shot
And flags have fallen into dust,
Your cross and mine shall tell men still
Christ died on each, for both of us.

For in the wreckage of your April Christ lies slain,
And Christ weeps in the ruins of my spring:
The money of Whose tears shall fall
Into your weak and friendless hand,
And buy you back to your own land:
The silence of Whose tears shall fall
Like bells upon your alien tomb.
Hear them and come: they call you home.

EVENING: ZERO WEATHER

Now the lone world is streaky as a wall of marble
With veins of clear and frozen snow.
There is no bird song there, no hare's track
No badger working in the russet grass:
All the bare fields are silent as eternity.

And the whole herd is home in the long barn.
The brothers come, with hoods about their faces,
Following their plumes of breath
Lugging the gleaming buckets one by one.

This was a day when shovels would have struck
Full flakes of fire out of the land like rock:
And ground cries out like iron beneath our boots

When all the monks come in with eyes as clean as the cold sky
And axes under their arms,
Still paying out Ave Marias
With rosaries between their bleeding fingers.

We shake the chips out of our robes outside the door
And go to hide in cowls as deep as clouds,
Bowing our shoulders in the church's shadow. lean and
                                         whipped,
To wait upon your Vespers, Mother of God!

And we have eyes no more for the dark pillars or the freezing
                                         windows,
Ears for the rumorous cloister or the chimes of time above
                                         our heads:
For we are sunken in the summer of our adoration,
And plunge, down, down into the fathoms of our secret joy
That swims with indefinable fire.

And we will never see the copper sunset
Linger a moment, like an echo, on the frozen hill
Then suddenly die an hour before the Angelus.

For we have found our Christ, our August
Here in the zero days before Lent—
We are already binding up our sheaves of harvest.
Beating the lazy liturgy, going up with exultation
Even on the eve of our Ash Wednesday,
And entering our blazing heaven by the doors of the
                              Assumption!

VASSAR MILLER

NO RETURN

Once over summer streams the ice-crusts harden,
No one can wade therein to wash his feet
Thence to go flying after nymphs that fleet
Naked and nimble through the woods. Time's warden
Has locked them all (or is it us?) past pardon.
Yet freed, we could not find the path that beat
Toward—call it any name—fauns, home, retreat;
For there is no returning to that garden.

No, not to Adam's. We must keep our own,
Remembering. In Eden's greenery
God walked. While in our garden rocks are brown
With His dried blood where He has crouched to groan.
Our apples rotted, only His crosstree
Bears crimson fruit. But no hand plucks it down.

PARADOX

Mild yoke of Christ, most harsh to me not bearing
You bruise the neck that balks, the hands that break you;
Sweet bread and wine, bitter to me not sharing,
You scar and scorch the throat that will not take you;
Mount where He taught, you cripple feet not bloody
From your sharp flints of eight-fold benediction;
Bright cross, most shameful stripped of the stripped body,
You crucify me safe from crucifixion:
Yet I, who am my own dilemma, jolting
My mind with thought lest it unthink its stiffness,
Rise to revolt against my own revolting.
Blind me to blindness, deafen me to deafness.
So will Your gifts of sight and hearing plunder
My eyes with lightning and my ears with thunder.

HOWARD NEMEROV

BOOM!

SEES BOOM IN RELIGION, TOO

Atlantic City, June 23, 1957 (AP).—President Eisenhower's
pastor said tonight that Americans are living in a period of
"unprecedented religious activity" caused partially by paid
vacations, the eight-hour day and modern conveniences.

"These fruits of material progress," said the Rev. Edward
L. R. Elson of the National Presbyterian Church, Washing-
ton, "have provided the leisure, the energy, and the means
for a level of human and spiritual values never before
reached."

Here at the Vespasian-Carlton, it's just one
religious activity after another; the sky
is constantly being crossed by cruciform
airplanes, in which nobody disbelieves
for a second, and the tide, the tide
of spiritual progress and prosperity
miraculously keeps rising, to a level
never before attained. The churches are full,
the beaches are full, and the filling-stations
are full, God's great ocean is full
of paid vacationers praying an eight-hour day
to the human and spiritual values, the fruits,
the leisure, the energy, and the means, Lord,
the means for the level, the unprecedented level,
and the modern conveniences, which also are full.
Never before, O Lord, have the prayers and praises
from belfry and phonebooth, from ballpark and barbecue
the sacrifices, so endlessly ascended.
It was not thus when Job in Palestine
sat in the dust and cried, cried bitterly;
when Damien kissed the lepers on their wounds
it was not thus; it was not thus
when Francis worked a fourteen-hour day
strictly for the birds; when Dante took

94

a week's vacation without pay and it rained
part of the time. O Lord, it was not thus.

But now the gears mesh and the tires burn
and the ice chatters in the shaker and the priest
in the pulpit, and Thy Name, O Lord,
is kept before the public, while the fruits
ripen and religion booms and the level rises
and every modern convenience runneth over,
that it may never be with us as it hath been
with Athens and Karnak and Nagasaki,
nor Thy sun for one instant refrain from shining
on the rainbow Buick by the breezeway
or the Chris Craft with the uplift life raft;
that we may continue to be the just folks we are,
plain people with ordinary superliners and
disposable diaperliners, people of the stop'n'shop
'n'pray as you go, of hotel, motel, boatel,
the humble pilgrims of no deposit no return
and please adjust thy clothing, who will give to Thee,
if Thee will keep us going, our annual
Miss Universe, for Thy Name's Sake, Amen.

MOMENT

Now, starflake frozen on the windowpane
All of a winter night, the open hearth
Blazing beyond Andromeda, the sea-
Anemone and the downwind seed, O moment
Hastening, halting in a clockwise dust,
The time in all the hospitals is now,
Under the arc-lights where the sentry walks
His lonely wall it never moves from now,
The crying in the cell is also now,
And now is quiet in the tomb as now
Explodes inside the sun, and it is now
In the saddle of space, where argosies of dust
Sail outward blazing, and the mind of God,
The flash across the gap of being, thinks
In the instant absence of forever: now.

JOHN FREDERICK NIMS

LETTER

Dear blonde, my twelve-month folly, loved no more,
This letter to you from my extreme shore,
Very remote—yes, hell-and-gone; no place
Mined with the cartridge memory of your face.
Forgotten the nights of blanket-twisted bed,
The intense revolver cried-for at my head
(Mostly when drunk); the kisses soft with mint;
Stray hair and lipstick and such lover's-lint.

Rarely I now remember what you were:
Eyes morning-clear and buckwheat-colored hair;
A child and stormy, fragile, fond of scotch,
Bartender's friend or newsboy's, no one's much;
Empty of love as glassware, often cruel
Only as babies are that dribble gruel.

Memory, once forged in fire and bear-trap hard,
Loses you now. Unless, old echoes heard,
I hold you (some other in my real arms caught)
One moment in a soft clasping of thought.
Seeing you board that downtown bus alone,
Little glass figure in a world of stone.

LOVE POEM

My clumsiest dear, whose hands shipwreck vases,
At whose quick touch all glasses chip and ring,
Whose palms are bulls in china, burs in linen,
And have no cunning with any soft thing

Except all ill-at-ease fidgeting people:
The refugee uncertain at the door
You make at home; deftly you steady
The drunk clambering on his undulant floor.

Unpredictable dear, the taxi driver's terror,
Shrinking from far headlights pale as a dime
Yet leaping before red apoplectic streetcars—
Misfit in any space. And never on time.

A wrench in clocks and the solar system. Only
With words and people and love you move at ease.
In traffic of wit expertly manoeuvre
And keep us, all devotion, at your knees.

Forgetting your coffee spreading on our flannel,
Your lipstick grinning on our coat,
So gayly in love's unbreakable heaven
Our souls on glory of spilt bourbon float.

Be with me, darling, early and late. Smash glasses—
I will study wry music for your sake.
For should your hands drop white and empty
All the toys of the world would break.

NED O'GORMAN

ON SAINT THERESA'S DIFFICULTY
IN KEEPING HER FEET ON THE GROUND

She would not leap for joy
and told her nuns employ
what means they must
to keep her close to dust.

But God would not obey
and when she went to pray
he picked her up
hood, bib and all and cut

the cloister up with levitation.
She stationed nuns, gravitation
guards she called them,
a wimpled group of ten

to guard her when she knelt.
They waited; at a nod (she felt
her heels kick up) they bound
her with a length of hemp, sound

to a boulder in the wall
and held her tight. But all
for nothing; loose or trussed
they could not keep the just

from rising to the ceiling.
They had a spanish feeling
that perhaps they guarded evil
in that cell. Who pulled? Keel

over once and diabolus perhaps
would roll his eyes; slaps
and knocks of imps; a screech
of angels filled out her peach

with boils; but when she prayed
she felt balloons and strayed
into the light. She roared
and from a line of pillars poured

the guardian ten and pulled
her back to earth. Hauled
down they slid her to a chair
and staked her there

with chains into the floor.
But settled down she was tore
up again and took
on high as fishers hook

a drowsing trout out of his den.
She fought the catch; when
Christus pulled her up she let
her shoulders drop; set

her teeth on edge and fell
at the knees. If it were hell
then hell it was; but she knew
that only God would argue

on the bias; leaving tit for tat
and standing up to all that
leverage, she told the carpenters
to pry her up and loose her center's

howling gravity. No more riot
balked her rising up. In the quiet
of halls of nunnery they saw
their mother floating grandly through the door.

READING DANTE WITH IONIANS

We did him, boys, with no care,
mucking through all that light
with our boots unlaced, right
into the face of God. We learned
the rhetoric of hell
and watched the celestial
flower wagon standing in the sun.

O my boys. All those things:
the sweet style of the world and
the unmaking of the mind; the land
of milk and honey, of roaring
kennels and lovers come to love
like cranes hovering above
a burning barn, pushed from nests

into the kinetic blast; the land
lying like a pulley between heaven
and hell, the leaven
of the sun and the racket of seraph.
We cannot tell how much we said,
how near we got to the head
and husk of the sanctified, but we

tried, O boys how we did try and never,
no matter if we're priest
or sybarite, husband or the least
dandy in the world's garden, will we know
again the bowl of heaven where the flow
and stammer of the Lord pitched
on the mind, how from this poem we learned

the possibilities of praise.

A HOMAGE TO MY JEWISH STUDENTS
AT CHRISTMAS TIME

In New England, a quiet place
with no extravagance of race
to hallow it, I tended toward
manner and repose, went schooling
in an ancient house and dreamed
of deer and crocuses. (Noah
would have left me in the rain
for I confused my sweetness
with my blood and thought the deer
lovelier than the mind.)

Guarded by the lion on our silver
crest I stalked through fields of lilies
in a sable sun to find my fantasies'
repose. (Though once I heard
that Moses drew fresh water from
a rock and thought that men of such
intent must be considerably divine.)

In our house God walked the ceilings
as a spider walks the undersides
of beams, or fire chimes out noon
on the sundial's face.
                            But you brought
God to me unspelled and reasoned
with my decorous intent and in this season
of Yahweh's stock I hear severing
Judith and the salts in my blood
build effigies and burning villages
and I think of the time God was on
mountains and division swam the sea.

ALFRED W. PURDY

WHO DOES NOT UNDERSTAND

Midnight in Troy. The hour when the legend split,
And Troilus dragged off by obedient Achilles
Also loved an imaginary Cressida, that
Girl and Helen whose warm welcoming bellies
Tempered medieval steel and stung the renaissance
And raffish Elizabethan studs with itching loins.
Well, we do exaggerate, perhaps. But once
There were women who stuck long pins
In men, pricked nerves, slashed pride and shrivelled egoes,
Who mirror-dazzled drove their beauty through
The dry, sealed centuries—whose damp bedroom sagas
Bewitched kings, butchers (and eunuchs, one scholar says).

And so, my dear: when the hot breath whistles
At midnight in the bedroom, give thanks and pray
For the secret statue another Leonardo chisels,
And the lovers who might have lost each other so easily.

ADRIENNE CECILE RICH

LIVING IN SIN

She had thought the studio would keep itself;
no dust upon the furniture of love.
Half heresy, to wish the taps less vocal,
the panes relieved of grime. A plate of pears,
a piano with a Persian shawl, a cat
stalking the picturesque amusing mouse
had risen at his urging.
Not that at five each separate stair would writhe
under the milkman's tramp; that morning light
so coldly would delineate the scraps
of last night's cheese and three sepulchral bottles;
that on the kitchen shelf among the saucers
a pair of beetle-eyes would fix her own—
envoy from some black village in the mouldings . . .
Meanwhile, he, with a yawn
sounded a dozen notes upon the keyboard,
declared it out of tune, shrugged at the mirror,
rubbed at his beard, went out for cigarettes;
while she, jeered by the minor demons,
pulled back the sheets and made the bed and found
a towel to dust the table-top,
and let the coffee-pot boil over on the stove.
By evening she was back in love again,
though not so wholly but throughout the night
she woke sometimes to feel the daylight coming
like a relentless milkman up the stairs.

RAYMOND ROSELIEP

FOR A SEVENTY-FIFTH BIRTHDAY

Against the night my world will feather-
shake when the last breath of you has dropped
its syllable on me, my mother,
and you will be younger than I hoped.

I come running with berry buckets
damp from woodgrass and the passed meadow,
a pocketful of active crickets,
and a myth about them to read you:

a son is a boy is an ocean
of wine stored in soils of his loving;
a manchild is the child in motion
faster than a field song caught and sung.

I come leaping against the structure
of Novembers shortening the years,
at your table become a fixture
where candles in a diamond pierce.

THE DAY MY FATHER WAS BURIED

My father died and I said part of me
is dead. I peeled some willow twigs. Until
I saw a tanager streaking our grass
with fire. And I wanted to shout indoors
and tell my mother all about it and
undo the darkness at our supper hour.
But death is quiet like the kitchen or
my mother's eyes, so I would not disturb
the still life of her house.

                    On the porch I
brooded, and lost my appetite. Until
I was again distracted . . .

And I would
not mention at the table that I felt
all right—lest I upset my mother's solitude or call attention to the lack
she must have known just then—

though I had seen
a bluejay with the sky upon his back.

OVER ELEMENTS

Now that I have surrendered, God (who
would not to your tameless cry? though they
call you a lamb), and the victory
over gusty elements that go
into the making of this manshape
gathers peace not constructed by hand,
and we have joined in a common bond. . . .

I must endeavor simply to grope
for the figures a child will shower
naming the giver and gift, or find
a word in the Canticle lover
to rally the gentle air and bring
from the brain's own shelter the lion
out of the house of Juda roaring.

ERNEST SANDEEN

CHILDREN OF MEN

I. GIRL THREE YEARS INTO THE WORLD

The love half-dreaming through me feels like laughter
Merely because she's so much smaller, warmer, softer,
Sleeping along my side, than any bosom lover

I've had or could have had. Her knuckles dimple
In parodies of women's hands, her face a simple
Little stratagem of health before the ample

Mind of beauty ripens. Let God have praise
For loaning me this love of her that laughs and plays
In the dozing silence of moments before the sun's full rise

To balance my other love of her, its twin
Who for her sake grieves all day for the world she's in
Dark with calamity and the evil made by children of men.

II. ECCE HOMO

The man who would beat a baby girl to death
Is alive. You have seen him wish his face
Away with handcuffed hands writhing beneath
Your stare of cameras. Numbered in your census
He hid his years among you to be a witness
Should time flash open to that abyss of love
Beyond your sounding which prophets suffered to tell you of.

And now your anger gathers before the courthouse
To protest the horror of yourselves his deed
Has found in you. Lifting placard and voice
You demand justice evict him from your blood
Even if in exchange the judge release
The Son of Man among you. And yet what good
Will come of this? Up from being dead

Behold the man bequeath his Pentecost
Of tongues, and now what child of man may not be lost.

LAST THINGS

I

The blow that felled him left my father's one
Hard hand lying as limp as a cast-off glove
Of leather. Now it was for me the son,
By a logic that overwhelmed us both, to shave
His harsh old face each day he had to live.
Revulsive my fingers explored the abyss of love

We'd carefully kept between us, and touched as tender
A skin as a baby girl's. A pain of wonder
Struck and flashed among the ages lost
In silent accumulations behind my back.
My ignorant fingers sparkled with the cost
He'd paid for anger vigilant to attack,

Not sparing wife and child who could hurt the most.
In the city of friends, so subtle was their approach,
He'd had to erect the barricades of reproach.
Yet for all his rage, with a shield as thin as his
I admired the luck he'd needed in having lost
Only a hand, war being what it is.

II

There came the last day of my father's breathing
When there was nothing, nothing to do except
To suffer time which suffered to a close.
I stared across his bed with rage seething
Through me at how the trees he'd planted slept
Outside our window permitting the fact of snows

To settle cold upon them and around
Them. Stupid they stood while the ashes of desolation,
Falling, reached and never reached their ground.
Anger as thick as blood was my consolation
For the storm of silence bleaching breath and space
Since nothing strong and tall out there had grace

Enough to toss defiance or even to bend
Before this beginning of memory and its end.

PATERNITY

My sons have casual powers given by love
To haunt my daytime with phantoms of who they'll be.
Yet none of these is the hero-by-night I dream of.
Under darkness and other rude disguises
I detect an older ghost of mine, who rises
Drunk as desire, yet only misbehaves
Like the guileless child he is and looks for, the boy
My parents buried alive in both their graves.

Without this desperate champion I might succumb
To the brute demanding cries that wrench my sons
To shape them in the image of love to come.
As day by day their fate grows in their eye
So day by day in their surmise I die.
But I am sick at the vengeance my hurt may find:
I feel their specters fumbling my skeleton
For those expected loves they left behind.

WINFIELD TOWNLEY SCOTT

FRIDAY SO SOON

There were many people on the island
Though, looking back at it now, it seems we were
Mostly alone together; we were allowed
The customary two weeks; the first
Floated like a slowed dream, like those boats
Windless and weightless and mirrored
Within folded lusters of air. The sea—
It is strange how at once on the island
You forget sea as the way of travel: others'
Continual arrival and disappearance
Enclosed us—safely, we thought, while
The sea-way which bore and must take us
Became God's moat to keep us.
We played in and out of it repeatedly.
Along shore that grass we almost sank in.
Weather spiralled from the full moon: storm
Shot rain and spray in salt horizontals
Three days. There was that too. Yet afterwards
The evening star like a pinwheel nail
Set all the galaxies awhirl until
Our island spun among them —
And then the sun with its wide quietness
Covered the sky and sea. The last days
Grew tense with being last: for instance,
Time and desire for swimming nearly vanished. We
Looked from sea at the grass and trees and flowers.
We were stilled by a recollected plan.
Sometimes I think I must have imagined it all
And yet how real you seemed when we ran with the sea.

WINFIELD TOWNLEY SCOTT

THE BLUE TREE

The leaves fell all from the tree.
The birds flew into it
And made for a while a blue tree.
They were jays—sarah and pinon jays:
Could perch intensely blue
And fly it intenser still:
Out they went as on strings
Circling, clustering in again.
Green the tree had been; then gold—
For days gold; now a moment blue.

Winter was beginning to come.
Snow on the mountains. From houses
All the blue doors in the wind clapped
"Hail Mary! Hail Mary!"
The sun sang like wires everywhere.
I, in another's dream—a strange country
Which belonged to me though not I to it:
I could speak, but got no answers.

If I grow old—I came to know this—
The world I die from can never be
The world most mine. Green given,
Gold from green; but then
The blue, temporary tree.
To love is to stay, and that
Will have been another place and season.
The tree flies green to somebody's other dream.

ANNE SEXTON

FOR GOD WHILE SLEEPING

Sleeping in fever, I am unfit
to know just who you are:
hung up like a pig on exhibit,
the delicate wrists,
the beard drooling blood and vinegar;
hooked to your own weight,
jolting toward death under your nameplate.

Everyone in this crowd needs a bath.
I am dressed in rags.
The mother wears blue. You grind your teeth
and with each new breath
your jaws gape and your diaper sags.
I am not to blame
for all this. I do not know your name.

Skinny man, you are somebody's fault.
You ride on dark poles—
a wooden bird that a trader built
for some fool who felt
that he could make the flight. Now you roll
in your sleep, seasick
on your own breathing, poor old convict.

UNKNOWN GIRL IN
THE MATERNITY WARD

Child, the current of your breath is six days long.
You lie, a small knuckle on my white bed;
lie, fisted like a snail, so small and strong
at my breast. Your lips are animals; you are fed
with love. At first hunger is not wrong.
The nurses nod their caps; you are shepherded
down starch halls with the other unnested throng
in wheeling baskets. You tip like a cup; your head

moving to my touch. You sense the way we belong.
But this is an institution bed.
You will not know me very long.

The doctors are enamel. They want to know
the facts. They guess about the man who left me,
some pendulum soul, going the way men go
and leave you full of child. But our case history
stays blank. All I did was let you grow.
Now we are here for all the ward to see.
They thought I was strange, although
I never spoke a word. I burst empty
of you, letting you learn how the air is so.
The doctors chart the riddle they ask of me
and I turn my head away. I do not know.

Yours is the only face I recognize.
Bone at my bone, you drink my answers in.
Six times a day I prize
your need, the animals of your lips, your skin
growing warm and plump. I see your eyes
lifting their tents. They are blue stones, they begin
to outgrow their moss. You blink in surprise
and I wonder what you can see, my funny kin,
as you trouble my silence. I am a shelter of lies.
Should I learn to speak again, or hopeless in
such sanity will I touch some face I recognize?

Down the hall the baskets start back. My arms
fit you like a sleeve, they hold
catkins of your willows, the wild bee farms
of your nerves, each muscle and fold
of your first days. Your old man's face disarms
the nurses. But the doctors return to scold
me. I speak. It is you my silence harms.
I should have known; I should have told
them something to write down. My voice alarms
my throat. "Name of father—none." I hold
you and name you bastard in my arms.

And now that's that. There is nothing more
that I can say or lose.
Others have traded life before
and could not speak. I tighten to refuse
your owling eyes, my fragile visitor.
I touch your cheeks, like flowers. You bruise
against me. We unlearn. I am a shore
rocking you off. You break from me. I choose
your only way, my small inheritor
and hand you off, trembling the selves we lose.
Go child, who is my sin and nothing more.

LOUIS SIMPSON

THE MAN WHO MARRIED MAGDALENE

The man who married Magdalene
Had not forgiven her.
God might pardon every sin . . .
Love is no pardoner.

Her hands were hollow, pale and blue,
Her mouth like watered wine.
He watched to see if she were true
And waited for a sign.

It was old harlotry, he guessed,
That drained her strength away.
So gladly for the dark she dressed,
So sadly for the day.

Their quarrels made her dull and weak
And soon a man might fit
A penny in the hollow cheek
And never notice it.

At last, as they exhausted slept,
Death granted the divorce,
And nakedly the woman leapt
Upon that narrow horse.

But when he woke and woke alone
He wept and would deny
The loose behavior of the bone
And the immodest thigh.

WILLIAM JAY SMITH

MISERERE

The lights have gone out in the School for the Blind.
    And all the shades are drawn.
    Sisters of Mercy move over the lawn.

Sisters of Mercy move into the mind
    With steps that are swifter than any;
    Light on each pupil is perched like a penny.

The lights have gone out in the School for the Blind;
    The flare on the runway dies,
    And the murderer waits with dancing eyes.

The murderer waits in the quiet mind,
    While Night, a Negress nun,
    A Sister of Mercy, sweeps over the sun.

LACHRYMAE CHRISTI

Let the redbird come to feast.
The cherry-pickers long have ceased.
And I can see their ladders there
All aslant the summer air,
Heavy on the shining trees.
They bear away the jewel box
With steps like fingers winding clocks
That have not ticked for centuries.
Time is dead: there is no time
No one now can ever climb
The ladder back to that black bough.
One man did, and he is dead;
And all the woods around are red.
And through the trees the redbirds fly,
While the rain falls from the cold sky.

FABLE FOR BLACKBOARD

Here is the grackle, people.
Here is the fox, folks.
The grackle sits in the bracken. The fox
  hopes

Here are the fronds, friends,
that cover the fox.
The fronds get in a frenzy. The grackle
  looks.

Here are the ticks, tykes,
that live in the leaves, loves.
The fox is confounded,
and God is above.

WORSHIP

Lofting fungoes at the rose
window of a church of elms,
evening worshipers with bat and ball
praise beyond idolatry that force
they, their symbols, and their act embody.
Morning worshipers with cap and shawl
bodied forth in off-to-market Fords
bump and haggle down the same
never-desecrated aisles.

Noon is lone: its worshiper
feels his chapel of gray flesh
lit and musicked by the jewelled elms
telling sun across his helpless hands.
Sunday all break worship, knock to church
grave as guilt can grin, to try stiff thoughts

116

on ungainly wood or word, and all,
feeling virtue leave them, cry
mea culpa, but sit tight.

MAY SWENSON

ORDER OF DIET

1

Salt of the soil and liquor of the rock
is all the thick land's food and mead.
And jaws of cattle grip up
stuffs of pasture for their bellies' need.
We, at the table with our knives,
cut apart and swallow other lives.

2

The stone is milked to feed the tree;
the log is killed when the flame is hungry.
To arise in the other's body?
Flank of the heifer we glut, we spend
to redden our blood. Then do we send
her vague spirit higher? Does the grain
come to better fortune in our brain?

3

Ashes find their way to green;
the worm is raised into the wing;
the sluggish fish to muscle slides;
eventual chemistry will bring
the lightning bug to the shrewd toad's eye.
It is true no thing of earth can die.

4

What then feeds on us? On our blood
and delectable flesh: the flood
of flower to fossil, coal to snow,
genes of glacier and volcano,
and our diamond souls that are bent
upward? To what Beast's intent
are we His fodder and nourishment?

PETER VIERECK

MOUNT ATHOS

The archimandrites in their mountain niches
    Are calling one another;
Like bells in separate steeples, each outstretches
    His bronze tongue to his brother.

On Macedonian hills these abbots kneel
    And rock till hilltops sway.
A goat-herd shudders as his pastures reel:
    "The archimandrites pray!"

Their beds are coffins, and their shirts are shrouds;
    They gash their palms with spears.
While virgin Angels simper from the clouds.
    "Our lovers are so fierce!"

Each archimandrite squats on his own peak
    And bellows at the skies.
Their beards are black and oily, long and sleek.
    And blow towards Paradise.

These burly priests (for patience far too proud)
    Roar out at death's delay;
Their hairy claws are flexed and gouge at God
    To speed his judgment day.

Above Mount Athos, cranes (a migrant swarm
    From Egypt to the Alps)
Are snatched in flight; their blood is guzzled warm
    In wild convulsive gulps;

And then (beyond endurance drunk with lust)
    The archimandrites spill
Their sainthood out: through wombs of clouds they thrust
    Their tautness, tall with Will.

119

Straight up to heaven—where their earth-love spews.
  Then fluttering Angel squads,
Calmed again, fold their wings, but now their eyes
  Fall when they meet God's.

WILFRED WATSON

LINES: I PRAISE GOD'S MANKIND IN AN OLD WOMAN

I praise God's mankind in an old woman:
I hear him rattle the body of an old wife
Dry and brown, and bitter as bracken,
Her stalk womb-cancelled, sere with seedgone;
With shrivel fingers clutching upon her life,
Wrestling for the empty pod and the dry leaf.
But still in her mildewed eyes moist's last token—
But oh, ever in her eyes the flash and strife,
Husk edge, cruel and sharp as any knife
Which not God's death itself can unsharpen.
Not all the frosts marching to this last March
Frost, not all the suns flaming to August
The last, dry-dried her spirit to adust;
She her own frost and sun at last must
Fetch—to blaze within and her soul's spirit parch
Into a desert—her own contracted flame;
Her radical sin, this sin at last to tame.
May she like the fathers by the desert broken
In her own desert find at last salvation.

RICHARD WILBUR

LOVE CALLS US TO THE THINGS
OF THIS WORLD

The eyes open to a cry of pulleys,
And spirited from sleep, the astounded soul
Hangs for a moment bodiless and simple
As false dawn.
                Outside the open window
The morning air is all awash with angels.

Some are in bed-sheets, some are in blouses,
Some are in smocks: but truly there they are.
Now they are rising together in calm swells
Of halcyon feeling, filling whatever they wear
With the deep joy of their impersonal breathing;

Now they are flying in place, conveying
The terrible speed of their omnipresence, moving
And staying like white water; and now of a sudden
They swoon down into so rapt a quiet
That nobody seems to be there.
                      The soul shrinks

From all that it is about to remember,
From the punctual rape of every blessèd day,
And cries,
        "Oh, let there be nothing on earth but laundry,
Nothing but rosy hands in the rising steam
And clear dances done in the sight of heaven."

Yet, as the sun acknowledges
With a warm look the world's hunks and colors,
The soul descends once more in bitter love
To accept the waking body, saying now
In a changed voice as the man yawns and rises,

"Bring them down from their ruddy gallows;
Let there be clean linen for the backs of thieves;
Let lovers go fresh and sweet to be undone,
And the heaviest nuns walk in a pure floating
Of dark habits,

               keeping their difficult balance."

Philippe de Thaun: T H E P E L I C A N

P E L L I C A N U S is the word
    For a certain breed of bird
Who truly is a crane;
    Egypt is his domain.
There are two kinds thereof;
    Near to the Nile they live;
One of them dwells in the flood,
    The fishes are his food;
The other lives in the isles
    On lizards, crocodiles,
Serpents, and stinking creatures,
    And beasts of evil nature.
In Greek his title was
    Onocrotalos,
Which is *longum rostrum,* said
    In the Latin tongue instead,
Or *long-beak* in our own.
    Of this bird it is known
That when he comes to his young,
    They being grown and strong,
And does them kindly things,
    And covers them with his wings,
The little birds begin
    Fiercely to peck at him;
They tear at him and try
    To blind their father's eye.
He falls upon them then
    And slays them with great pain,

Then goes away for a spell,
    Leaving them where they fell.
On the third day he returns,
    And thereupon he mourns,
Feeling so strong a woe
    To see the small birds so
That he strikes his breast with his beak
    Until the blood shall leak.
And when the coursing blood
    Spatters his lifeless brood,
Such virtue does it have
    That once again they live.

K N O W that this pelican
    Signifies Mary's Son;
The little birds are men
    Restored to life again
From death, by that dear blood
    Shed for us by our God.
Now learn one meaning more,
    Revealed by holy lore:
Know why the small birds try
    To peck their father's eye,
Who turns on them in wrath
    And puts them all to death.
Men who deny the light
    Would blind God's blazing sight,
But on such people all
    His punishment will fall.
This is the meaning I find;
    Now bear it well in mind.

AN EVENT

As if a cast of grain leapt back to the hand,
A landscapeful of small black birds, intent
On the far south, convene at some command
At once in the middle of the air, at once are gone
With headlong and unanimous consent
From the pale trees and fields they settled on.

What is an individual thing? They roll
Like a drunken fingerprint across the sky!
Or so I give their image to my soul
Until, as if refusing to be caught
In any singular vision of my eye
Or in the nets and cages of my thought,

They tower up, shatter, and madden space
With their divergences, are each alone
Swallowed from sight, and leave me in this place
Shaping these images to make them stay:
Meanwhile, in some formation of their own,
They fly me still, and steal my thoughts away.

Delighted with myself and with the birds,
I set them down and give them leave to be.
It is by words and the defeat of words,
Down sudden vistas of the vain attempt,
That for a flying moment one may see
By what cross-purposes the world is dreamt.

JAMES WRIGHT

FATHER

In paradise I poised my foot above the boat and said:
Who prayed for me?
                            But only the dip of an oar
In water sounded; slowly fog from some cold shore
Circled in wreaths around my head.

But who is waiting?
                      And the wind began,
Transfiguring my face from nothingness
To tiny weeping eyes. And when my voice
Grew real, there was a place
Far, far below on earth. There was a tiny man—

It was my father wandering round the waters at the wharf.
Irritably he circled and he called
Out to the marine currents up and down,
But heard only a cold unmeaning cough,
And saw the oarsman in the mist enshawled.

He drew me from the boat. I was asleep.
And we went home together.

COME FORTH

Lazarus lay to see the body turn.
The femur first removed itself from arms,
The elbows folded under each other soon.

The clavicle and vertebrae and shin
Divided like the stars and let the air
Caress the flesh awake before it fell.

Only the torpid brain would not remove.
From far away beyond the granite walls
A vowel of longing tore the wind in two.

Come forth, it said. *But who is this who cried?*
For I have left the human long ago,
My flesh a synagogue the flame has eaten.

Before the voice the worms began to pray,
And fled away howling into the granite.
The shin returned to spring a leaping leg.

The skull rounded itself upon the brain,
The heart arose and cried with joy for pain.
The arteries assumed a thud again.

And the hair furied on the shocking head,
And muscles blossomed like the thunderhead
That trumpets the pale tropics to green storm.

The stones rolling away and the air thrust
Into the lung of the cave, Lazarus knew
The unholy and indifferent sting of wind

Across the flesh of man. Outside, the sun
Flayed the same bone as before. Nevertheless
His treading skeleton clattered like a choir

And waved him forward on a crest of praise.
A wall or two away the calling voice
Shook like a pacing father, and was still.

O blessed fire, O harsh and loving air.

MUTTERINGS OVER THE CRIB OF A DEAF CHILD

"How will he hear the bell at school
Arrange the broken afternoon,
And know to run across the cool
Grasses where the starlings cry,
Or understand the day is gone?"

Well, someone lifting curious brows
Will take the measure of the clock.
And he will see the birchen boughs
Outside sagging dark from the sky,
And the shade crawling upon the rock.

"And how will he know to rise at morning?
His mother has other sons to waken,
She has the stove she must build to burning
Before the coals of the nighttime die;
And he never stirs when he is shaken."

I take it the air affects the skin,
And you remember, when you were young,
Sometimes you could feel the dawn begin,
And the fire would call you, by and by,
Out of the bed and bring you along.

"Well, good enough. To serve his needs
All kinds of arrangements can be made.
But what will you do if his finger bleeds?
Or a bobwhite whistles invisibly
And flutes like an angel off in the shade?"

He will learn pain. And, as for the bird,
It is always darkening when that comes out.
I will putter as though I had not heard,
And lift him into my arms and sing
Whether he hears my song or not.

DATE DUE